E

In *Why You've Been Duped Into Believing that the World is Getting Worse*, J.D. King presents verifiable research and well-documented statistics that demolish the myth that the world is disintegrating. King makes it clear that the gospel of God's Kingdom is prevailing globally. This is a brilliant work that restores hope to a hopeless society.

—STEVE GRAY

Author of *When The Kingdom Comes: Lessons From the Smithton Outpouring*, Senior Pastor of World Revival Church in Kansas City

For us Baby Boomer Christians who grew up on *The Late Great Planet Earth*, the future was deliciously and fascinatingly evil. J.D. King, in his latest book, asserts that we have been "duped" by this gloomy view of the future. Via numerous documented metrics, King shows that the influence of Christian values—and the growth of Christianity itself—is raising the quality of life around the globe. Thank you, J.D., for this provably optimistic worldview.

—JON MARK RUTHVEN, PhD.

Author of *On the Cessation of the Charismata* and *What's Wrong with Protestant Theology*, Professor Emeritus, Regent University

What I love about anything J.D. King brings to the table is that you can expect to receive an engaging synergy of scholarship and spiritual insight. I'll be completely up front: I do not know if my end-times theology is in complete harmony with J.D.'s. And you know what? That's okay! I am convinced that every believer needs to wrap their collective thinking around the data J.D. presents in this timely book. Whether you believe

Jesus will return imminently, at "any moment," or otherwise, I'm convinced there is a commission for the Ekklesia, the church that Jesus commissioned, to leave society better.

This book is a charge for all believers to be salt and light, while rejecting the fear-mongering and sensationalism that is often associated with imbalanced eschatology. The idea that the church will experience "Great glory" and revival, while the world grows increasingly dark is actually incompatible with who Jesus call us to be—salt and light. If we are salt and light, then we need to have a measurable impact on the world we have been placed in. If we are salt and light, then we should leave society better than it was prior to our entry and influence.

I'm convinced that the Kingdom of God is an ever-increasing Kingdom. How does this ever-increasing Kingdom have an ever-increasing impact and influence on the world? Through carriers of the Kingdom - the people of God - fulfilling their assignments in every sphere of influence. It's not enough to simply be optimistic about the future; we need to recognize that the future should be shaped by the Kingdom of God. *Why You've Been Duped Into Believing that the World is Getting Worse* is a charge for you to become the change you want to see in the Earth!

—LARRY SPARKS
Author of *Arise, Breakthrough Faith, Ask for the Rain,* and *The Fire That Never Sleeps,* Publisher for Destiny Image, lawrencesparks.com

Why You've Been Duped into Believing that the World is Getting Worse is a must read! While many point out problems in our world, J.D. King does an amazing job presenting the other side of the story—providing information and actual data. J.D. does not deny that bad things are happening; he just wants us to know there's more to this story. Even as evil remains in our world, the Kingdom of God is boldly advancing. I hope that this book will change minds. The ultimate sign of the increasing Kingdom isn't merely the absence of evil, but a mature, fruitful church ready to receive Jesus as He returns.

—DUSTIN SMITH

Worship albums: *Miracles: The Healing Project, and Only A Holy God*

Integrity Music Recording Artist

Jesus commanded us not to worry about tomorrow, yet I meet so many Christians who are terrified about where our world is headed. Paul said to "be joyful always" and "never stop giving thanks," yet I continually see a misunderstanding of the world's condition rob Christians of their joy, while the only future thing they're thankful for is that one day Jesus will rescue them out of it. How sad this is when we realize it's completely unnecessary! Contrary to what the ratings-driven media will tell you (remember, fear sells), J.D. King lays out a brilliant, scholarly case for the gradual improvement of our world (and most importantly, the Gospel-mechanism behind it all). You're living at the greatest time in history, and those who embrace the worry-free joy and gratitude available in Christ can be part of this world-improving family called 'the Church.' The Media may have duped us, but this book will set the record straight. Read it, and start changing the world.

—ART THOMAS

Missionary-evangelist, author, and filmmaker,

www.SupernaturalTruth.com

J.D. King has written an encouraging, engaging, and perspective changing book about how the Kingdom of God is advancing in the earth! Faith and Hope are its clear message. He opens a refreshing window of fact-based reality that confronts unbelief, ignorance, and indifference. *Why You Have*

Been Duped into Believing that the World is Getting Worse has stirred me to fresh faith and courage. I agree with the author, Jesus is winning in the nations!

—DAMON CHANDLER

Instructor, Director of Student Mobilization, International House of Prayer University, Kansas City

In his new book, J.D. King reveals that things are getting better in the world. Just as Jesus, in his first miracle, produced the best wine at the end, it makes sense that the Lord has saved the best for last! Unfortunately, the enemy has "duped" many Christians, into thinking the opposite. With Jesus' teaching, "your kingdom come, your will be done on as it is in heaven," he was revealing that the atmosphere of heaven can be brought into every realm of life. With that, it is impossible for things to get worse.

I highly recommend *Why You've Been Duped into Believing that the World is Getting Worse*. It will encourage you and give you the courage to bring the atmosphere of heaven to your family, your workplace, and your church!

—DANNY W. SEAY

CEO—G458 Holdings, LLC—U.S.A., Chief Business Development Officer—Global Business Initiative, Inc—South Africa, Executive Vice President—XRPetroleum—Australia

This book is epic in its scope—yet easy to read in its style. J.D. King has basically done the boring stuff for you—he has researched and gathered facts and information from a variety of sources and presented it in an exciting and engrossing read. This book provides concrete evidence that the world is progressing, that life is improving, that problems are declining, and Christianity is growing. In pointing all this out, it is preparing us for the continued advancement of God's great plan.

—MARTIN TRENCH

Co-Author of *Victorious Eschatology*

Although much of Christendom believes that things are growing worse, J.D. King contends for the opposite viewpoint in his eye-opening and faith-building new book, *Why You've Been Duped into Believing that the World is Getting Worse*. Moving beyond sensationalism and fear, this book provides solid statistical evidence from respected researchers and scholars. While many believe that things are moving in the wrong direction, King reveals that life on earth is actually getting better. Now we can all breathe a little easier.

—BRENT RUDOSKI

Author of *Mercy Triumphs Over Judgment*, Senior Pastor of Faith Alive Family Church, Saskatoon, Canada

The writer of Ecclesiastes puts the past in perspective when he writes: "Do not say, 'Why is it that former days were better than these?' For it is not from wisdom that you ask about this" (Ecclesiastes 7:10).

Bad things are happening in the world. No one would dispute this. There were bad things happening in the first century and every century thereafter. The so-called "good old days" weren't always that good, but Christians made future days better.

There are a lot of good things happening in our day, as J.D. King points out in his fact-filled book *Why You've Been Duped into Believing that the World is Getting Worse*. The gospel can be sent around the world at the speed of light. People affected by natural disasters can be reached within days instead of weeks or months. There are hospitals within driving distance of most people in the United States and other developed nations.

The Bible has been translated into most languages. Many translations are online—for free! There is no need to smuggle Bibles in some countries if an internet connection is available.

Until the invention of the locomotive, the speed of transportation was no faster than a horse. Can you imagine what living conditions would be like today if we were literally using horse power?

When you finish reading J.D.'s book, there is only one question you will need to answer: "How will I deal with the challenges God puts in front of me?"

—GARY DEMAR
Author of *Last Days Madness* and *Wars and Rumors of Wars*

WHY YOU'VE BEEN

DUPED

INTO BELIEVING THAT THE WORLD IS GETTING WORSE

J.D. King

Christos Publishing

Blessings

Christos Publishing
Post Office Box 1333
Lee's Summit, Missouri 64063

For Worldwide Distribution

Printed in the United States of America
First Printing, January 2019

ISBN 978-0-9992826-5-6

While all stories in this book are true, some names and identifying information have been changed to protect the privacy of the individuals involved.

DEDICATION

For Allyson, Matthew, and those privileged to inherit creation.

"The gentle are blessed,
for they will inherit the earth."

(MATTHEW 5:5)

ACKNOWLEDGMENTS

Books worth reading aren't birthed in isolation. They're part of the overflow of meaningful conversations and relationships. A whole tribe of people shapes what's written.

That was certainly the case with me when it came to this book. I'm indebted to friends and colleagues who helped with this project. They enabled a tiny seed to grow into a mighty oak.

Most importantly, I want to acknowledge Bobbie, my marvelous confidant and partner. She has not only sacrificially supported my writing efforts, but she has also provided treasured counsel. I know that I would be lost without my beautiful wife.

Steve and Kathy Gray, pastors of World Revival Church in Kansas City, also deserve recognition. From the beginning, they supplied invaluable guidance. Their encouragement and wisdom remain monumental in my life.

I'm also grateful for colleagues who offered constructive analysis and editorial guidance. The fingerprints of Aaron Lage, J.A. Hardgrave, Art Thomas, Amy Schmidt, and Elizabeth McKinley-Tuttle are found throughout the pages of this work.

I want to acknowledge the insights of Stephen Pinker, Hans Rosling, Max Roser, Gregg Easterbrook, Johan Norberg, and Matt Ridley. This manuscript draws heavily from their well-documented writings. While I do not agree with all their conclusions, I'm indebted to their research.

No one genuinely walks alone. Our insights and impressions are always part of a broader realm of community. I'm grateful for the support of so many. I continue to be overwhelmed by their abundant generosity.

TABLE OF CONTENTS

Foreword | i

Introduction | v
Why this Story Needs to be Told

Section One

1. It's the End of the World as We Know it | 1
Cultural Anxiety and the Fear of the Unknown

2. What We've Got Here is Failure to Communicate | 7
Worldview, Media, and the Apocalypse

3. Cry Havoc, and Let Slip the Dogs of War | 15
Casualties of War, Terrorism, and Murder

4. Do Not Go Gentle into that Good Night | 29
Disease, Life Expectancies, and Infant Mortality

5. As God is My Witness, I'll Never Be Hungry Again | 41
Poverty, Malnourishment, and Basic Needs

6. Fight the Power | 57
Sexual Assault, Racism, and Injustice

7. In the Gaps Between the Stories | 73
   Why the World is Getting Better

Section Two

8. Continuous as the Stars that Shine | 87
   Christianity's Inexplicable Wonder

9. I Bless the Rains Down in Africa | 97
   Christianity's Expansion in Africa

10. Burning Ring of Fire | 107
    Christianity's Expansion in Latin America

11. An East Wind Blowing | 115
    Christianity's Expansion in Asia

12. The Desert is an Ocean | 123
    Christianity's Expansion in the Middle East

13. All is Quiet on the Western Front | 131
    Christianity's Expansion in North America and Europe

14. Even Darkness Must Pass | 143
    Concluding a Marvelous Journey

For Further Reading | 149

Questions for Review and Group Discussion | 153

You Can Help! | 163

FOREWORD

We live in an age where, at any hour of the day, we can be inundated with fear-filled news about the state of our world. J.D. King's book, *Why You've Been Duped*, challenges that mindset. With a wealth of accurate statistics on his side, King goes toe-to-toe with the pervasive message of hopelessness, revealing the difference between facts and lucrative sensationalism. A world headed towards ruin might sell more papers, but King brilliantly proves that our world is not deteriorating. It is advancing. And it is advancing through the effectiveness of the gospel. Ultimately, King is not just asking the reader to be convinced by his research; he is inviting us to believe the Word of God. "Of the increase of His government there will be no end." Jesus is returning for a glorious Bride, one who has fulfilled His mandate to go to all of the earth, discipling nations until the world looks like heaven. Things are getting better. There is hope. The end of the story has already been written, and (spoiler alert) the kingdom of God wins. If ever we needed a book of this nature, it is now.

—BILL JOHNSON
Author of *When Heaven Invades Earth* and
The Supernatural Power of a Transformed Mind,
Senior Leader of Bethel Church, Redding, California

"What you see and what you hear depends a great deal on where you are standing. It also depends on what sort of person you are."

—C.S. Lewis

INTRODUCTION

WHY THIS STORY NEEDS TO BE TOLD

"Be strong and take heart,
all you who hope in the Lord."

(PSALM 31:24 NIV)

This book began as an extended blog post. I had collected articles, analyzing what was happening in the world. Some clippings were in an email inbox and others stuffed in a desk drawer. I knew that I had to pull this information together in a single form so that I could better process it. Sometimes I do my best thinking while writing.

I started writing an article for my own personal benefit but quickly recognized its potential to help others. Although the research and writing took several days to complete, I didn't mind. I was thankful that I had the time to process these essential matters.

After I finished, I posted the article, imagining that it would only get a few hundred page views—after all, it was long and riddled with footnotes. People don't typically respond well to that kind of writing. Little did I know that this article would become the most widely circulated piece that I had ever written.

I uploaded the article link to social media feeds. Within an hour, it received one hundred likes and twenty shares on Facebook. On Twitter, dozens were linking to it. Although most agreed with it, criticism also arose.

In one instance, two longtime friends took me to task. One said that he believed that I was deceiving the masses. The other told me that I didn't know anything about the end times. He exclaimed, "J.D., you are utterly confused about what God is up to in the world."

I had apparently touched a nerve. Some thanked me for what I wrote, grateful for a little hope. Others told me that I didn't understand the Bible or world events. In the midst of the controversy, people kept reading and sharing the article.

Over the next week, the post shockingly raced around the globe. Hundreds reposted it on Facebook, Twitter, and Reddit. Charisma Media contacted me about publishing it on their online forum. By the end of the month, a quarter of a million people had read my article. I couldn't believe the level of exposure the article had received; it was unfathomable to me.

When I traveled to a conference and spoke at an out-of-town church, people asked about the post. Some high-profile leaders that I admire contacted me. A significant prayer conference asked if my research could be used as a basis for a keynote session. I later found out that an influential Christian recording artist had been following my blog. The reach of my write up went beyond my wildest expectations.

I've wanted to expand this material and put it into an accessible book form for several years. But with family needs and work responsibilities, I struggled to find the time.

Whenever this project came up, I told myself that I'd pick it up later. But all that changed after I received an email in early 2018.

An acquaintance that I had lost track of wrote me and asked for the link to my original post. He explained that my article had transformed his thinking and encouraged him to move forth in victory in his Christian walk.

For the first time in years, he was able to cast off anxiety and fear. His whole world was transformed as he re-embraced the hope of the gospel.

His email reminded me that many are in a similar place. While despair grips the lives of multitudes, it doesn't have to. The world can be framed and genuinely re-envisioned other ways.

That is why I wrote this book. *You've Been Duped into Believing that the World is Getting Worse* is an invitation to see things differently and to change your perspective about what is happening.

Under divine inspiration, Solomon declared, "Hope deferred makes the heart sick, but a dream fulfilled is a tree of life" (Proverbs 13:12 NIV). He reminded those who want to triumph that hopelessness is not an option.

What happened to my friend can happen to you. Move beyond the anxiety and fear. Read the following pages and awaken hope. God is up to amazing things in the world, and you can align yourself with his plans now.

This life is much more than misery and despair. God hasn't forgotten us or left us to our own devices. His goodness and love are transforming the cosmos.

SECTION ONE

"I must study politics and war that my sons may have liberty to study mathematics and philosophy. My sons ought to study mathematics and philosophy, geography, natural history, naval architecture, navigation, commerce, and agriculture, in order to give their children a right to study painting, poetry, music, architecture, statuary, tapestry, and porcelain."

—President John Adams (1735-1826)

1. IT'S THE END OF THE WORLD AS WE KNOW IT
CULTURAL ANXIETY AND THE FEAR OF THE UNKNOWN

"If the blind lead the blind, both will fall into a pit."

(MATTHEW 15:14 NIV)

A friend of mine named Michael revealed his unease about the mounting violence in the Middle East. He was particularly concerned about the vicious onslaught by an Islamic organization known as ISIS.

This terrorist group that originated as part of al Qaeda in Iraq has expanded throughout the Arab world. Part of its rapid advancement includes brutalizing and beheading anyone countering its violent form of Islamic fundamentalism.

Reflecting on frightening news reports, my friend exclaimed, "Anyone with half a brain can see that the world is getting progressively worse. Evil is advancing around us, and the Christian church is losing ground. It's impossible to turn a blind eye to how bad things are getting."

I was saddened to see my friend immobilized by fear. You would not expect to observe anxiety about the future in a dedicated follower of Jesus Christ. It is contrary to our identity and mandate. The Bible says, "Don't worry about anything; instead, pray about everything" (Philippians 4:6 NLT). We are advised to fill our lives with goodness and hope. Yet so many embrace anxiety and fear.

Hopeless Fatalism

Many churchgoers are overwhelmed by hopeless fatalism. Anxiety engulfs the stadiums, department stores, and pews. Multitudes are convinced the world is in free-fall, and it's only a matter of time before the apocalypse. Untold masses believe that America is on the eve of destruction.

With social media updates and images on television, people readily assume that the world is getting worse. The media overwhelms us with anarchies, epidemics, and financial collapses. On TV, it isn't hope—but despair—that springs eternal.

Decades ago, Paul Ehrlich, a Stanford University researcher, declared on The *Tonight Show* that "sometime within the next 15 years the end will come."[1] More recently, a journalist in The *New York Times* said that people "have never previously felt so uneasy about the state of the world."[2] With Nazi and totalitarian regimes breathing down necks in the past, it's hard to comprehend why anyone would suggest this.

Apparently media personalities believe that the earth is on the edge of annihilation and that life is worse than ever before. Matt Ridley bemoans,

> The airwaves are crammed with doom. In my own adult lifetime, I have listened to implacable predictions of growing poverty, coming famines, expanding deserts, imminent plagues, impending water wars, inevitable oil exhaustion, mineral shortages, falling sperm counts, thinning ozone, acidifying rain, nuclear winters, mad-cow epidemics, Y2K computer bugs, killer bees, sex-change fish, global warming, ocean acidification and even asteroid impacts that would presently bring this happy interlude to a terrible end. I cannot recall a time when one or other of these scares was

[1] Paul Ehrlich quoted in Clyde Haberman, "The Unrealized Horrors of Population Explosion," *New York Times* (May 31, 2015).

[2] Roger Cohen, "A Climate of Fear," *New York Times* (October 27, 2014).

not solemnly espoused by sober, distinguished and serious elites and hysterically echoed by the media.[3]

After being bludgeoned with pessimism season after season, men and women are convinced that society and the very earth itself are unraveling. Forty years of analysis confirms that every year a majority of Americans believe the country is heading in the wrong direction.[4] Steve Dunning observes,

> When a recent survey asked "All things considered, do you think the world is getting better or worse?" the results were predictably bleak. In Sweden, only 10% thought things are getting better, and in the U.S., it was only 6%. Hardly anyone thinks the world is getting better.[5]

You can easily see where the doomsayers are coming from. With unsettling images of bloodshed, who could doubt evil's unmitigated growth? Societal collapse appears to be a self-evident truth.

My friend, Michael, certainly felt this way. He apprehensively asked, "What kind of life is there going to be for my children?" He was convinced that the future was grim.

[3.] Matt Ridley, *The Rational Optimist: How Prosperity Evolves* (San Francisco: HarperCollins, 2010), 280.

[4.] See Steven Pinker, *Enlightenment Now: The Case for Reason, Science, Humanism, and Progress* (New York, Penguin Publishing, 2018), 40.

[5.] Steve Denning, "Why The World Is Getting Better And Why Hardly Anyone Knows It," *Forbes* (November 2017).

This dire outlook is pervasive, but is it accurate? Are evil forces rapidly expanding across the globe? Is humanity descending into greater chaos and destruction in the twenty-first century?

Making An Assessment

How do we determine whether cynicism is justified? Are there any reasonable standards of analysis? Steven Pinker, a cognitive scientist and Pulitzer Prize-winning author, posed the following in response to this question,

> How can we soundly appraise the state of the world? The answer is to count. How many people are victims of violence as a proportion of the number of people alive? How many are sick, how many starving, how many poor, how many oppressed, how many illiterate, how many unhappy?[6]

If the world is getting worse, shouldn't there be higher rates of illiteracy, racism, and gender inequality? In a deteriorating society, violence would likely be increasing. The statistics should be observable and speak for themselves.

[6.] Steven Pinker, *Enlightenment Now: The Case for Reason, Science, Humanism, and Progress* (New York, Penguin Publishing, 2018), 42-43.

Before claiming that society is collapsing, shouldn't we establish a baseline? What do statistics reveal? Surely a survey of relevant data could show whether things are declining?

This discussion should include cumulative global statistics. One cannot argue that the entire world is getting worse and only consider the United States. The earth is made up of more than one people group.

Fear Can't Take Us Anywhere

A sense of dread grips so many people. My friend Michael got entangled in this. As he anxiously declared that terrorism was growing, panic seemed to intensify.

I said that just because life felt a certain way did not mean that those emotions were valid. I could tell that he didn't like the direction of the conversation, and tensions rose. I pressed in regardless, explaining that fear doesn't always take us where we want to go.

I explained that God was up to beautiful things in the world and that we shouldn't lose hope. Reality and our perceived sense of events aren't always the same. We have never heard some parts of this unfolding story.

My friend and I talked about many things that day. I felt that some of what we discussed would benefit others as they delve into what is actually happening in the world. Reality is considerably different than many people imagine. It's time to pull back the curtain and see what's going on in the cosmos.

2. WHAT WE'VE GOT HERE IS FAILURE TO COMMUNICATE

WORLDVIEW, MEDIA, AND THE APOCALYPSE

"Since ancient times no one has heard, no ear has perceived, no eye has seen any God besides you, who acts on behalf of those who wait for him."

(ISAIAH 64:4 NIV)

Whenever I journey back to Arkansas, the overwhelming beauty of the Ozarks strikes me. Magnificent forests overtake the horizon along the rugged peaks and underground streams.

As a young boy, I stared out the back window of my parent's car, barely noticing the majestic terrain as we drove the winding roads. The old, familiar backdrop didn't seem worthy of attention. It didn't occur to me that grandeur was hidden in plain sight.

Sometimes we miss what is right in front of us. Anxiety, fear, and small-mindedness can easily obscure our view. We are so enamored with the unimportant that we miss what's vital.

Astonishing beauty lies within the created order. Nevertheless, many struggle to see it. Multitudes only grasp what they have been programmed to recognize. They don't pay attention to positive advancements. Hans Rosling, a Swedish statistician, declared,

> It is easy to be aware of all the bad things happening in the world. It's harder to know about the good things: billions of improvements that are never reported.[1]

Pessimism is Big Box Office

In the spring of 2018, a group of college students berated some Kansas City businessmen. They claimed that truth and virtue were their only motivations, but their attacks felt more like totalitarian programming. We shouldn't allow hollow pop culture to have such a great influence.

---

[1] Hans Rosling with Ola Rosling and Anna Rosling Rönnlund, *Factfulness: Ten Reasons We're Wrong About the World—and Why Things Are Better Than You Think* (New York, Flatiron Books, 2018), 51.

Insightful analysis and poignant storytelling is admired. Yet hidden agendas lie below the surface. I want to believe the students' earnestness but have a hard time getting past their calculated methods.

Beneath the claims of objectivity, most influencers see themselves as activists. They relish being so-called watchdogs, muckrakers, whistleblowers, and afflicters of the comfortable.[2]

Media pundits are aware that they're powerless without the attention of the masses, and in the theater of imagination, "pessimism has always been big box office."[3]

Looking away from a mangled train wreck is hard. Curiosity grips our imagination. With the inescapable pull of catastrophe, gatekeepers persuasively accentuate the negative. Pinker points out that

> Media scholars who tally news stories of different kinds, or present editors with a menu of possible stories and see which they pick and how they display them, have confirmed that the gatekeepers prefer negative to positive coverage.[4]

[2] See Steven Pinker, *Enlightenment Now: The Case for Reason, Science, Humanism, and Progress* (New York, Penguin Publishing, 2018), 49.

[3] Matt Ridley, *The Rational Optimist: How Prosperity Evolves* (San Francisco: HarperCollins, 2010), 294.

[4] Steven Pinker, *Enlightenment Now: The Case for Reason, Science, Humanism, and Progress* (New York, Penguin Publishing, 2018), 42.

Editors and programming directors operate by the adage, "If it bleeds, it leads."[5] They eagerly exploit the innate human instinct to notice the bad more than the good. Eric Weiner, a prominent radio broadcaster, writes, "The truth is that unhappy people, living in profoundly unhappy places, make for good stories."[6] Anxieties stir up crowds and fatten the bottom line of global corporations.

Commentators love to tell us where the world is going wrong, setting up narratives as skirmishes between opposing people or views. Extreme poverty is, for example, contrasted with the opulent lifestyles of billionaires. With the skill of a novelist, they "pit the fragile individual against the big, evil corporation."[7]

Social media mavens can't avoid ramping up the rhetoric. Rosling says that almost every activist "exaggerates the problem to which they have dedicated themselves."[8] If money must be raised, highlight the apparent problem. People don't pay attention to resolved crises. Matt Ridley writes,

> No charity ever raised money for its cause by saying
> things are getting better. No journalist ever got the
> front page by telling his editor that he wanted to

---

[5] Deborah Serani, PSY.D., "If It Bleeds, It Leads," *Psychology Today* (June 2011).

[6] Eric Weiner, *The Geography of Bliss: One Grump's Search for the Happiest Places in the World* (New York: Twelve, 2008), 1.

[7] Hans Rosling with Ola Rosling and Anna Rosling Rönnlund, *Factfulness: Ten Reasons We're Wrong About the World—and Why Things Are Better Than You Think* (New York, Flatiron Books, 2018), 38-39.

[8] Ibid., 189.

write a story about how disaster was now less likely. Good news is no news, so the media megaphone is at the disposal of any politician, journalist or activist who can plausibly warn of a coming disaster.[9]

Journalists and newscasters know that pessimism sells. So newspapers and television broadcasts focus on conflict. The stories are riddled with selective reporting, highlighting only what they want people to hear.

Government policymakers warn of global crises, and cultural architects frighten people "with alarmist exaggerations and prophecies."[10] While insisting that everything is falling apart, they exhibit only a fragment of what's transpiring in the world.

The fact that our distracted culture is frequently misled shouldn't surprise us. Considerable advantage can be gained from the confusion. Less scrupulous politicians and religious authorities want you agitated. Fearful people are easier to manipulate and control.

A pessimistic storyline unconsciously entangles innocent people. They dance to dreadful songs that squelch their passion and reinforce the suffocating rule of oppressors.

---

[9] Matt Ridley, *The Rational Optimist: How Prosperity Evolves* (San Francisco: HarperCollins, 2010), 295.

[10] Ibid., 67-68.

Embracing A Dark Narrative?

An older gentleman once asked me, "If pessimism is such a mistaken viewpoint, why do so many buy into it? If this outlook permeates our culture, surely there's something to it. How could the outcomes be so drastically distorted?"

Many assume that the truth rises to the surface, but this is not always so. For a variety of reasons, society often fails to see what is actually occurring.

One culprit is humanity's inclination to remember events inaccurately. People romanticize the past and scorn the future, particularly as they age. One's childhood was never as ideal as remembered and the future never as ominous.

Nothing is more responsible for the so-called "good old days" than a bad memory. Johan Norberg writes,

> Many have sensed a connection between this idealization of the past with the idealization of our lost childhood, the nostalgic wish to return to a state of security and excitement. As we get older, we take on more responsibility, we sometimes get disillusioned or bored, and a certain decay of physical capacity sets it. It is easy to mistake changes in ourselves with changes in the times.[11]

[11.] Johan Norberg, *Progress: Ten Reasons to Look Forward to the Future* (United Kingdom: One world Publications, 2016), 214.

Nostalgia and distorted memories are not our only problems. Oppressive religious narratives are also at work. Harsh doctrinal systems obscure positive advancements. Entangled in rigid dogma, some insist that the earth is heading for cataclysm. One can't have hope and also contend that everything will be obliterated.

More is at work than revisionism and religious cynicism. Our pessimism also comes from a place of deep, personal struggle. Tragedies often result in a negative bias. Since individuals frame the world by generalizing first-hand experiences, a divorce or death negatively influences one's worldview.

Conflating your world with the world as a whole is normal. What happens to you feels like the fate of the cosmos. But all of us need to be reminded that what's felt might not represent the entirety of life.

Beauty Along the Periphery

With all the sensationalism and abrasiveness, it's hard to imagine an improving world. Good seems implausible. Yet promising developments cannot be ignored.

From the vantage point of the present, almost all of history's trends take us in a positive direction. Around the globe, violence, disease, and poverty are lessening. The unfolding annals of history reveal an optimistic story.

I understand that many will discard this assertion. It conflicts with cherished assumptions and long-held stories. I don't think anyone likes the idea that they're wrong about what's happening in the world. But sometimes we don't see as clearly as we think we do.

People have seemingly valid reasons for rejecting hope. Disappointments come from all directions. Adverse circumstances disrupt well-ordered lives. I do not deny the unsettling reality of problems. Difficulties will come. Nevertheless, things are never as bad as they seem.

As I mentioned at the beginning of this chapter, I was recently transfixed as I drove back to Arkansas. I thought to myself, "How could I have missed this? Who in their right mind overlooks such breathtaking landscapes?" It occurred to me that it's easy to ignore what's in front of you when you're preoccupied with the wrong stories.

Along the periphery, beauty and wonder are overtaking the world. Marvelous realities are emerging. It's time to take another look. Try to see things as they are—not just how they're depicted. What's currently happening in our world is better than we have ever imagined.

3. CRY HAVOC, AND LET SLIP THE DOGS OF WAR:
CASUALTIES OF WAR, TERRORISM, AND MURDER

*"They will beat their swords into plowshares and
their spears into pruning hooks. Nation will not
take up sword against nation, nor will they train
for war anymore."*

(ISAIAH 2:4 NIV)

A few years ago, I grabbed coffee with an aging Vietnam vet. Decades after his tour of duty, concealed wounds still remained. The ravages of war caused more than bodily harm. They burrowed into his mind and emotions.

Because this former soldier couldn't sleep and had flashbacks at the slightest provocation, his family struggled. After years of unresolved tension, his wife left him.

He not only mourned family and comrades who died on the battlefield, but also the loss of normalcy. He realized that although he made it home, part of him died in Southeast Asia.

With a solemn expression, he told me that what happened to him would happen to others. He believed that America was teetering on the edge of war and that conflict was inevitable.

I don't think that I will ever forget one of the things that he whispered. "War is an endless circle that society never actually escapes. Eventually, other mothers will weep over the spilled blood of their sons."

I was troubled by his words and wondered about their accuracy. Honestly, will every generation be dragged into war? Should Americans expect the bloodshed to continue?

Unimaginable violence shows up on social media. Across the globe, callous terrorist attacks appear. Homicides rock cities. Yet are these horrific acts growing in intensity? Are abysmal events overtaking our world?

Casualties of War

Across the annals of history, millions have been in entangled in violent conflict. The drumbeat of war resonates over land and sea. Bloodshed and atrocities seemed unending.

During the Medieval Crusades, over 1.7 million died,[1] and in the Mongolian invasions of Arabia, causalities were over 2 million.[2] Both bloodbaths occurred during a period when less than 400 million people walked the earth.

Centuries later, 20 million were slaughtered in the Taiping Rebellion (1850-1864).[3] During that same era, 750,000 died in the American Civil War (1861-1865).[4] Less than fifty years later, 9 million were slain during the Russian Revolution (1917-1922).[5] Finally, an unfathomable 117 million died in World Wars I and II.[6]

Until the 1940s, nations were continually in conflict. Western European countries initiated war every two or three years. Historian Arnold Toynbee, writing in the afterglow of the Second World War, declared, "In our recent Western history, war has been following war in an ascending order of intensity."[7] To his well-informed mind, the bloodshed was unceasing.

---

[1] Jay Michaelson, "Was Obama right about the Crusades and Islamic extremism?" *Washington Post* (February 6, 2015).

[2] Steven Pinker, *The Better Angels of Our Nature: Why Violence Has Declined* (New York: Penguin Publishing, 2011), 196.

[3] "Taiping Rebellion (1850-1864)," Columbia University, http://afe.easia.columbia.edu/special/china_1750_taiping.html.

[4] Guy Gugliotta, "New Estimate Raises Civil War Death Toll," *New York Times* (April 2, 2012).

[5] "Highest death toll from a civil war," *Guinness World Book of Records*, http://www.guinnessworldrecords.com/world-records/highest-death-toll-from-a-civil-war.

[6] See "World War I (1914-1918): Killed, Wounded, and Missing," *Encyclopedia Britannica*, https://www.britannica.com/event/World-War-I/Killed-wounded-and-missing.

[7] Arnold Toynbee, *War And Civilization* (New York: Oxford University Press, 1950), 4.

Most everyone was shocked as battles began to wane. War—understood as the uniformed armies of nation-states fighting—became virtually obsolete in recent decades. There have been less than four major conflicts in any year since 1945 and, in most years since 1989, there have been none.[8]

Along with fewer incidents of war, genocide and collateral deaths are plummeting. Pinker declares,

> By any standard, the world is nowhere near as genocidal as it was during its peak in the 1940s, when Nazi, Soviet, and Japanese mass murders, together with the targeting of civilians by all sides in World War II, resulted in a civilian death rate in the vicinity of 350 per 100,000 per year.[9]

Since the mid-twentieth century, genocide and civil strife have diminished drastically. War-related deaths are currently the lowest ever recorded. In the twenty-first century, only a tiny percentage of the global population has been maimed in conflict. Pinker notes,

> The rate of documented direct deaths from political violence (war, terrorism, genocide and warlord militias) in the past decade is an unprecedented few

---

[8.] Steven Pinker, *Enlightenment Now: The Case for Reason, Science, Humanism, and Progress* (New York, Penguin Publishing, 2018), 158.

[9.] Steven Pinker and Andrew Mack, "The World Is Not Falling Apart: Never mind the headlines. We've never lived in such peaceful times," *Slate* (December 2014).

hundredths of a percentage point. Even if we multiplied that rate to account for unrecorded deaths and the victims of war-caused disease and famine, it would not exceed 1%.[10]

It is easy to forget how violent our ancestors were. They lived in an unimaginably brutal world. This observation might seem absurd, but the past was drastically more appalling than the world we now reside in.

Global War Related Deaths, 1946-2016

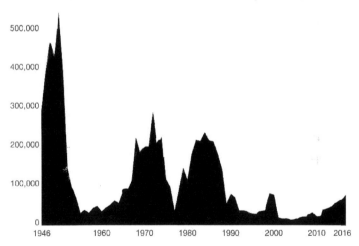

Source: Our World in Data

---

[10]. Steven Pinker, "Violence Vanquished," *The Wall Street Journal* (September 24, 2011).

Few, if any, in media will tell you this, but we might be living in the most peaceful time in the history of the world.[11] In fact, traffic accidents often take more lives than military conflicts. Gregg Easterbrook reminds us that "in the current generation, roads have been more dangerous than armies."[12]

Terrorism

As a minister, I often have conversations with people about their anxieties. I hear about the issues that keep them awake at night. From time to time, someone will bring up fears about war.

One businessman told me, "I'm not worried about military conflict —our government can handle that. What bothers me is terrorism. There's not a lot that can be done about unhinged radicals."[13]

I understood his sentiments. Highly publicized attacks from Islamic extremists ratchet up our anxieties. Americans are on edge as they contemplate being assaulted in another rampage killing. Reflecting on this common fear, Pinker writes,

> In 2016, a majority of Americans named terrorism
> as the most important issue facing the country.
> They said they were worried that they or a family

[11.] See C.J. Werleman, "We're living through the "most peaceful era" in human history—with one big exception," *Salon* (Wednesday, January 15, 2014).

[12.] Gregg Easterbrook, *It's Better Than It Looks: Reasons for Optimism in an Age of Fear* (New York: Public Affairs, 2018), 109.

[13.] A personal conversation with a used car dealer from Raytown, Missouri in early 2005.

member would be a victim, and identified ISIS as a threat to the existence or survival of the United States.[14]

After slaughtering thousands of innocent people, television cryptically portrayed ISIS and Boko Haram. The brutal beheadings gave the impression that terrorism was increasing around the world. Most don't realize that the number slain through terrorist acts is only a fraction of all who have been killed. Currently, 0.05 percent of annual deaths are attributed to radical extremism.[15]

Consider that the widely reported assaults of the shoe and underwear bombers were fruitless. The Tsarnaev brothers, assailants in the Boston Marathon bombing, maimed hundreds, but only managed to kill three.

Terrorist acts are often more about psychological warfare than enacting physical violence. Radicals want to ignite fear—not necessarily kill *en masse.*

Without minimalizing the impact of terrorism, those affected have been minuscule in comparison to the victims of other catastrophes. Although religiously motivated violence makes headlines, it represents a small fraction of deaths.

[14.] Steven Pinker, *Enlightenment Now: The Case for Reason, Science, Humanism, and Progress* (New York, Penguin Publishing, 2018), 191.

[15.] Hans Rosling with Ola Rosling and Anna Rosling Rönnlund, *Factfulness: Ten Reasons We're Wrong About the World—and Why Things Are Better Than You Think* (New York, Flatiron Books, 2018), 122.

Extremists have killed 3,172 Americans over two decades in heartbreaking attacks. We cannot make light of this. Nevertheless, this is, on average, only about 159 people a year.[16]

Statistics confirm that more Westerners die in bathtubs and from staircase falls than from Islamic violence.[17] People are afraid of things that they will likely never encounter. Fear—not violence per se—is driving radicalism's agenda.

Terrorist threats stir anxieties. Families harbor fear about the invasion of their neighborhoods. Most of these concerns are misplaced. Despite what we witness on television, religious violence isn't pervasive. In fact, it is decreasing.

Journalists from *Reuters* news service reported the following:

> The number of terrorist attacks worldwide and deaths from such attacks dropped in 2016 for the second straight year, driven by decreases in Afghanistan, Syria, Nigeria, Pakistan, and Yemen . . . . The total number of terrorist attacks in 2016 dropped 9 percent compared to 2015, while fatalities caused by the attacks fell 13 percent.[18]

[16.] Ibid., 121.

[17.] Various, *Human Security Report 2013* (Vancouver: Human Security Press, 2014), 25.

[18.] Various, "Number of Terrorist Attacks Globally Dropped in 2016: U.S. Government," *Reuters* (July 19, 2017).

It doesn't matter how the world looks on television or social media, Islamic fundamentalism isn't conquering the globe. Violence is diminishing, and fewer lives are being taken. Human brutality remains, but the world is moving in a peaceful direction.

Homicides

A little while back, I spoke with a man from Chicago. He described the horrendous murders taking place in his city. He said, "So many young men are dying that they don't even put it on the news anymore." He explained that homicide was perhaps the number one crisis in America.

It is easy to see where he was coming from. In the twenty-first century, fears about violent crime keep people awake at night. It is not just anxieties about terrorism and war but a sense that our children might be harmed.

In Gallup polls, over the last twenty years, at least two-thirds consistently believed homicides were increasing.[19] Many are convinced that murder rates are the highest ever recorded. But things are not as they seem.

Most don't realize that untamed violence prevailed in the past. Hans Rosling documented what archeologists found in the ruins of early civilizations.

[19.] John Gramlich, "5 Facts about Crime in the U.S.," *Pew Research Center* (January 30, 2018).

The truth is to be found in ancient graveyards and burial sites, where archeologists have to get used to discovering that a large proportion of all the remains they dig up are those of children. Most will have been killed by starvation or disgusting diseases, but many child skeletons bear the marks of physical violence. Hunter-gatherer societies often had murder rates above 10 percent and children were not spared. In today's graveyards, child graves are rare.[20]

It is hard to imagine living in a world where the homicide rate was 15 percent, but researchers have concluded that was the reality in some ancient societies. Bloodshed, in ages past, must have been unusually severe.[21]

In comparison to today, a medieval traveler was a hundred times more likely to be murdered in Italy.[22] During this era, Europeans encountered relentless brutality. Pinker writes,

Lords massacred the serfs of their rivals, aristocrats and their retinues fought each other in duels, brigands and highwaymen murdered the victims of

---

[20.] Hans Rosling with Ola Rosling and Anna Rosling Rönnlund, *Factfulness: Ten Reasons We're Wrong About the World—and Why Things Are Better Than You Think* (New York, Flatiron Books, 2018), 67-68.

[21.] See Johan Norgerg, *Progress: Ten Reasons to Look Forward to the Future* (United Kingdom: Oneworld Publications, 2016), 88.

[22.] Douglas T. Kenrick, Ph.D., "Ten Ways the World Is Getting Better: Steven Pinker, Science, Humanism, and Progress," *Psychology Today* (March 2018).

their robberies, and ordinary people stabbed each other over insults at the dinner table.[23]

In subsequent centuries, murderous acts decreased, and the civilized world became less violent. Lives were not taken as often as they were in previous generations.

Although homicide rates were tremendously high in the early American colonies, they plummeted in succeeding eras, reaching an all-time low in the late twentieth century.[24]

It is counterintuitive, but the FBI disclosed that homicides dropped nearly 50 percent in the last twenty-five years.[25] Murders are now less frequent in every region of the United States. While there are outliers like Chicago and St. Louis,[26] most cities are witnessing a marked reduction in gun violence.

Reflecting on positive changes in New York City, Gregg Easterbrook suggests that "Central Park after dark now is as safe as Yellowstone Park at noon."[27]

[23.] Steven Pinker, *Enlightenment Now: The Case for Reason, Science, Humanism, and Progress* (New York, Penguin Publishing, 2018), 168.

[24.] Max Roser, "Homicides," Our World In Data, https://ourworldindata.org/homicides

[25.] John Gramlich, "5 facts about crime in the U.S.," Pew Research Center (January 30, 2018). The homicide rate in the United States is now lower than five per 100,000. Manuel Eisner, "Long-Term Historical Trends in Violent Crime," *Crime and Justice* 30 (2003): 83–142.

[26.] Editor, "The 30 Cities with the Highest Murder Rate in the US," *Bismark Tribune* (November 13, 2017).

[27.] Gregg Easterbrook, *It's Better Than It Looks: Reasons for Optimism in an Age of Fear* (New York: Public Affairs, 2018), xvii.

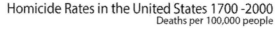

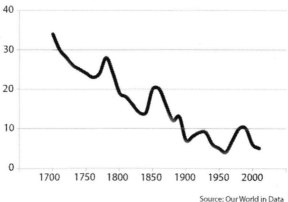

Homicide Rates in the United States 1700 -2000
Deaths per 100,000 people

Source: Our World in Data

The decline of violence isn't unique to the United States. Among eighty-eight countries with reliable data, sixty-seven reported fewer homicides over the last forty years.[28]

Contradicting the fear-inducing pessimism of the media, fewer than ever are dying from gunshots or stabbing. Against common assumptions, violence is plummeting across the globe. Pinker reminds us that

> There are 180,000 people walking around today
> who would have been murdered just in the last year
> if the global homicide rate had remained at its level
> of a dozen years before.[29]

---

[28] Various, "Homicide Declined in Most Nations," United Nations Office on Drugs and Crime. https://www.unodc.org/gsh/en/data.html.

[29] Steven Pinker, *Enlightenment Now: The Case for Reason, Science, Humanism, and Progress* (New York, Penguin Publishing, 2018), 171.

Diminishing Bloodshed

Although brutality continues, conflicts that kill hundreds aren't the same as wars slaughtering millions.[30] Bloodshed has dramatically decreased. But in spite of the advancements, the evening news still finds just enough violence to anchor every broadcast.

Sporadic catastrophes on the far side of the world continue to mar the worldview of a generation. Johan Norberg writes,

> War, crime, disasters and poverty are painfully real, and during the last decade global media has made us aware of them in a new way—live on screen, every day, around the clock—but despite this ubiquity, these are problems that have always existed, partially hidden from view. The difference now is that they are rapidly declining. What we see now are the exceptions, where once they would have been the rule.[31]

While we mourn the pain that remains, we must recognize that the world is considerably improved. There has never been a better time in all of history to be alive.

[30.] "The average interstate war killed 86,000 people in the 1950s and 39,000 in the 1970s. Today, it kills slightly more than 3,000 people." Johan Norberg, *Progress: Ten Reasons to Look Forward to the Future* (United Kingdom: One world Publications, 2016), 100.

[31.] Ibid., 48.

Occasionally I think of the Vietnam vet that I chatted with over coffee a few years ago. Because of what he and others like him fought for, this world sees less bloodshed. As I thanked him and told him that he was making the world more peaceful, a tear rolled down his face. Hope is rising in some of the most unexpected places.

4. DO NOT GO GENTLE INTO THAT GOOD NIGHT:
DISEASE, LIFE EXPECTANCIES, AND INFANT MORTALITY

"For the grave cannot praise you, death cannot sing
your praise; those who go down to the pit cannot hope
for your faithfulness."

(ISAIAH 38:18 NIV)

I was standing in the grocery store checkout line next to a young mother. While we waited, we engaged in a conversation about life and family. She told me that virtually every one of her relatives was sick. Most disturbingly, her father's body was ravaged with cancer.

As I prayed for her and tried to bring encouragement, she posed a heartbreaking question. "Is every family forced to contend with sickness? Are thousands of diseases just gestating in people's bodies, waiting to destroy everything?"[1]

She said that it was hard to see beyond the disease. The pain seemed insurmountable. Sensing her burden, I told her that circumstances would improve and that for most people, life was better than she imagined.

This exchange made me wrestle with some of my own questions. Is society experiencing an increase of disease in the twenty-first century? Are more dying from pandemics than ever before? Is it reasonable to be anxious about the threat of illness?

Disease

Across the globe, people are terrified of diseases. Warnings about illnesses are frequently reported in newspapers. Image-driven social media displays tainted food and exotic viruses. Many are convinced that mysterious diseases are taking over the world. This feverish outlook is hardly new.

In the January 1970 edition of *Life Magazine*, tens of thousands of subscribers would have encountered the following:

> Scientists have solid experimental and theoretical evidence to support . . . the following predictions: In a decade, urban dwellers will have to wear gas masks to survive air pollution . . . . By 1985 air

---

[1.] Conversation with unnamed woman at Price Chopper grocery store in Lee's Summit, Missouri on November 9, 2017.

pollution will have reduced the amount of sunlight reaching earth by one half . . . . New diseases that humans cannot resist will reach plague proportions.[2]

During subsequent decades, so-called experts warned of cosmetics containing toxic levels of lead, causing infertility, miscarriage, and brain damage.[3] Later, the masses became fearful about Severe Acute Respiratory Syndrome (SARS),[4] H5N1 (the bird flu),[5] H1N1 (the swine flu),[6] and Ebola.

Because of this blistering narrative, millions were frightened. Impressionable mothers believed that an unavoidable scourge was taking root in the world, endangering the lives of their children.

Fears about disease compel parents to keep their children indoors. Some shun polio, measles, and mumps vaccines, concerned that the cure might be worse than the disease.

[2.] Editor, "Ecology The New Mass Movement," *Life Magazine* 68:3 (January 30, 1970), 22.

[3.] See Dina El Boghdady, "400 Lipsticks Found to Contain Lead, FDA Says," *Washington Post* (February 14, 2012).

[4.] See Robert J. Blendon, John M. Benson, Catherine M. Des Roches, Elizabeth Raleigh, Kalahn Taylor-Clark, "The Public's Response to Severe Acute Respiratory Syndrome in Toronto and the United States," *Clinical Infectious Diseases* 38:7 (April 2004): 925–931.

[5.] See Rebecca Cook Dube, "Skeptics warn bird flu fears are overblown," *NBC News* (April 20, 2006).

[6.] See Jess Henig, "FactCheck: Swine Flu Vaccine Fears Greatly Exaggerated," *Newsweek* (October 18, 2009).

People wrongly assume that incidents of illness are increasing. Most don't realize that sickness was more prevalent in previous eras. The scope of disease in the twenty-first century is nothing compared to the past.

For example, over 30 percent of people in late medieval Europe died from the Black Death, a plague induced by a bacterium.[7] In the eighteenth, nineteenth, and twentieth centuries, smallpox killed at least half-a-billion people.[8] Over the last century, polio paralyzed and killed as many as five hundred thousand people annually.[9]

Illnesses are nowhere as severe in this generation as they were in the past. For the most part, our collective fears have been overblown. SARS, Ebola, the bird flu and other so-called global pandemics only had minimal impact.[10]

Other undeniable advances don't receive such widespread press. Smallpox has effectively ceased to exist,[11] and polio has been

---

[7.] See Suzanne Austin Alchon, *A Pest in the Land: New World Epidemics in a Global Perspective* (Albuquerque: University of New Mexico Press, 2003), 21. This infectious disease was caused by bacteria that spread in the air and by physical contact, and was carried by the fleas on rats.

[8.] J. N. Hays, *Epidemics and Pandemics: Their Impacts on Human History* (Santa Barbara, California: ABC CLIO, 2005), 151.

[9.] Various, *Canadian International Immunization Initiative* (September 2007), 3.

[10.] In 2005, the U.N. suggested that as many as 150 million people would die from the bird flu. It ended up being less than 300 people worldwide. See Matt Ridley, *The Rational Optimist: How Prosperity Evolves* (San Francisco: HarperCollins, 2010), 308-309.

[11.] Steven Pinker, *Enlightenment Now: The Case for Reason, Science, Humanism, and Progress* (New York, Penguin Publishing, 2018), 64-65.

drastically curtailed.[12] Maladies like malaria,[13] the measles,[14] and mumps,[15] have also plummeted.

Deaths due to cancer have fallen twenty-two percent[16] since 1994, and AIDs-related fatalities have been diminishing for the last fifteen years.[17] Make no mistake about it, illnesses are being pushed back.

Poilio Cases in America

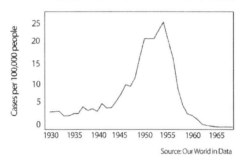

Source: Our World in Data

[12.] Ibid., 65.

[13.] Ibid., 66.

[14.] "Since the mid-1800s, measles is estimated to have killed about 200 million people. Several million died every year until a vaccine was made available in the early 1970s. Today, it results in around 100,000 deaths annually, a reduction of more than ninety-six per cent since the early 1980s." Johan Norberg, *Progress: Ten Reasons to Look Forward to the Future* (United Kingdom: One world Publications, 2016), 54.

[15.] Various, "Recommendations of the International Task Force for Disease Eradication," *Morbidity and Mortality Weekly Report* 42 (1993), 8.

[16.] Editor, "More than 1.5 million cancer deaths averted in last two decades," *CBS News* (December 31, 2014). The number of new cases of HIV/AIDS worldwide has been falling for a decade, and deaths from the disease has been falling since 2005. Matt Ridley, *The Rational Optimist: How Prosperity Evolves* (San Francisco: HarperCollins, 2010), 307-308.

[17.] Matt Ridley, *The Rational Optimist: How Prosperity Evolves* (San Francisco: HarperCollins, 2010), 307-308.

William Fogel, a Cambridge academic, observes, "Chronic diseases among Americans today are not just less severe than they were a hundred years ago, but they also begin an average of ten years later in life."[18]

Disease is still wreaking havoc, but health conditions are the best they have ever been in recorded history. The earth is unquestionably a more invigorating place.

Life Expectancy

I recently heard a woman insist that multitudes are being taken out in the prime of life. She contended that people aren't living as long as they used to, which was an indication that our world is collapsing.

This woman walked through tragedy, so I understand that personal experiences colored her outlook. Many have been affected by similar moments of heartbreak.

Several of my ancestors didn't live long. I knew neither of my grandfathers. One died a decade before I was born and the other when I was only five. I felt disconnected from family legacies because I didn't hear their stories.

When life feels a certain way, we can easily imagine that it's moving in the wrong direction. Negative encounters can be overly defining. Nevertheless, reality is more than the sum total of our experiences.

[18.] William Fogel, *The Escape From Hunger and Premature Death, 1700–2100: Europe, America, and the Third World* (Cambridge: Cambridge University Press, 2004), 10.

Contrary to what we've been told, life is not moving in a downward spiral. Rather than dying younger, people are living longer. I will likely get to know my grandchildren and great-grandchildren. For most of us, life will not be cut short.

When it comes to this discussion, we must consider the data. Facts, not feelings, must be the basis of dialogue. Statistics confirm that people have gradually enjoyed longer lifespans over the centuries.

Individuals in Ancient Greece and the Roman Empire could only enjoy a life expectancy of eighteen to twenty-five years of age.[19] As late as 1720, the average European still only lived thirty years. Most are now walking the earth considerably longer.

Max Roser, a gifted researcher at Oxford University, made the following observations:

> Estimates suggest that in a pre-modern, poor world, life expectancy was around 30 years in all regions of the world. In the early 19th century, life expectancy started to increase . . . . Since 1900 the global average life expectancy has more than doubled and is now approaching 70 years.[20]

[19.]Abdel R. Omran, "The Epidemiologic Transition: A Theory of the Epidemiology of Population Change," *Milbank Quarterly* 83:4 (2005): 731–57.

[20.] Max Roser, "Life Expectancy," *Our World in Data*, https://ourworldindata.org/life-expectancy

In less than a century, global life expectancies have expanded and are approaching eighty years of age. Across the earth, people have many more years to spend with their families.

Source: Our World in Data

Confounding common assumptions, analysts suggest that life expectancy in wealthier nations will surpass one hundred years of age in a few decades. Death keeps getting pushed back, and people enjoy more time with loved ones. Pinker declares, "No matter how old you are, you have more years ahead of you than people of your age did in earlier decades and centuries."[21]

Ample evidence of an improving world exists. What the media states is not necessarily accurate. For most, life keeps getting better.

[21.] Steven Pinker, *Enlightenment Now: The Case for Reason, Science, Humanism, and Progress* (New York, Penguin Publishing, 2018), 59.

Child Mortality

Another cause for concern is the premature death of babies. The loss of a precious child can feel like the shattering of the world. Families wonder how life can go on.

I have known several couples who have lost a baby. It grieves me to see the pain that they have to walk through. No mother and father should have to bury their child. That is not how life is supposed to work.

Tragedies happen, but it would be wrong to say that a higher percentage of children are dying. Reports confirm that more infants than ever are surviving and growing into adulthood.

Although far too many babies still die in the twenty-first century, infant mortality is nothing like it was. In the early nineteenth century, 40 percent of children died before the age of five.[22] Although this improved in later generations, an average family still suffered the death of at least one baby.[23]

On the eve of the twentieth century, every third child in Sweden never awoke, and in Germany, one out of every two.[24] Tremendous wailing spread through households as many lives were cut short.

People focus on present conditions but are unaware of the horrors of previous generations. Today, only half of one percent

---

[22.] Ibid.

[23.] Max Roser, "Child Mortality," *Our World in Data*, https://ourworldindata.org/child-mortality.

[24.] Ibid.

(0.5 percent) of kids in the United States and Europe are dying. When compared with the past, this is indeed a golden age.

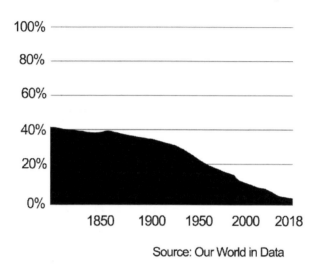

Global Child Mortality

Source: Our World in Data

Lower infant mortality speaks volumes about the beauty of our changing world. Hans Rosling clarified this, writing,

> When only 14 children die out of 1,000 in Malaysia, this means that the other 986 survive. Their parents and their society manage to protect them from all the dangers that could have killed them: germs, starvation, violence, and so on. So this number 14 tells us that most families in Malaysia have enough food, their sewage systems

don't leak into their drinking water, they have good access to primary health care, and mothers can read and write. It doesn't just tell us about the health of children. It measures the quality of the whole society.[25]

We should rejoice that there's not a single nation around the globe with a higher number of children dying. When fragile babies survive, society is working as it should. Lower infant mortality rates remind us that the earth is finally finding its rhythm.

No More Strangleholds

Hope is rising and beauty is emerging. As disease is losing its stranglehold on society, people are living longer and relishing the companionship of their families.

Don't let the media pundits and naysayers fool you—good things are transpiring. Considering the benchmarks that profoundly affect everyday life, billions have every reason to celebrate.

The woman in the grocery line that I mentioned earlier thanked me for expressing concern. At that time, she was desperate for hope. I ran into her months later at a restaurant. She mentioned that her father was doing better and that life no longer seemed so

---

[25.] Hans Rosling with Ola Rosling and Anna Rosling Rönnlund, *Factfulness: Ten Reasons We're Wrong About the World—and Why Things Are Better Than You Think* (New York, Flatiron Books, 2018), 20.

daunting. Her outlook and tone had changed, and she asked for my continued prayers.

Her story and others that I've heard remind me that the world is improving. The moment we are living in is filled with more goodness and joy. There has never been a better era to be alive.

5. AS GOD IS MY WITNESS, I'LL NEVER BE HUNGRY AGAIN

POVERTY, MALNOURISHMENT, AND BASIC NEEDS

*"Remember the LORD your God, for it is he who
gives you the ability to produce wealth, and so
confirms his covenant."*

(DEUTERONOMY 8:18 NIV)

Two young girls raced away as my father and I pulled up to my childhood church in rural Arkansas. They were drinking water from an outdoor spigot and were afraid that they would get in trouble.

My dad sensed that something was amiss and trailed after them to their house. When he knocked on the door, he discovered the family was struggling financially, and their water had been turned off.

My father drove to city hall and took care of the past-due bill. Not long afterward, we went to the grocery store and picked up food for them.

This experience left an indelible mark on my life. This act of generosity was perhaps one of the fondest memories that I have of my father. He demonstrated that the poor need our love and support.

Hunger and other problems persist. Yet we sometimes imagine that they are worse than they truly are. Compassion is essential, but the ugliness and despair are not nearly as pervasive as we think. People want to alleviate burdens, but they sometimes end up exasperating the problems.

I am acquainted with social justice activists who insist that the earth is gripped by poverty. They warn us that the global financial substructure is teetering on the verge of collapse.

Others frame an equally bleak outlook. As I scroll through my social media feed, I see photographs of malnourished children living in squalor. Captions scream that without a generous gift, this third-world village will never have access to clean water. Charitable work is essential, but I reject the assertion that a nation is hopeless without outside intervention. People often have viable solutions within their own culture.

On the home front, joblessness and a lack of resources seemingly haunt the urban core. Many insist that life is falling apart, and despair grips the multitudes. They believe that families will never have what they need to survive. Yet is this a right perspective?

Extreme Poverty

Families are struggling in our communities. I have personally encountered some underprivileged people in the Kansas City metro. I helped get an impoverished man into the City Union Mission, ensuring he had a bed and food. Although the poor remain among us, we mistakenly believe that their ranks are increasing.

The notion that the world is becoming destitute in the twenty-first century is widespread. Many are convinced that poverty rates are escalating. Steve Denning, a gifted analyst, observes,

> In both the United Kingdom and the United States, most people think that the share of people living in extreme poverty has increased! Two thirds in the U.S. even think the share in extreme poverty has "almost doubled."[1]

Is this contention accurate? Are economies truly failing? Will current financial trajectories create a breakdown for billions of people?

[1.] Steve Denning, "Why The World Is Getting Better And Why Hardly Anyone Knows It," *Forbes* (November 2017).

Although counterintuitive, humanity is currently entering a tremendously prosperous age. Instead of diminishment, economies are expanding. Some nations that are rich today were considered poor just a few decades ago.[2] More people than ever before have escaped abject poverty.

In earlier centuries, impoverished conditions subsumed every nation. Max Roser reiterates that

> Economic prosperity and lasting economic growth
> is a very recent achievement for humanity . . . .
> Incomes remained almost unchanged over a period
> of several centuries when compared to the increase
> in incomes over the last two centuries."[3]

Two hundred years ago, even the citizens of wealthy countries were destitute. At that time, only a privileged few weren't constrained by finances.[4] According to estimates, 94 percent of the world was penniless in 1820.[5]

Economic conditions did not overly change in succeeding years. Shockingly, over 50 percent of the world population was still

[2] Ibid.

[3] Max Roser, "Economic Growth," *Our World in Data,* https://ourworldindata.org/economic-growth.

[4] Steve Denning, "Why The World Is Getting Better And Why Hardly Anyone Knows It," *Forbes* (November 2017).

[5] Max Roser, "The Short History of Global Living Conditions and Why it Matters that we Know it," *Our World In Data.* https://ourworldindata.org/a-history-of-global-living-conditions-in-5-charts.

residing in extreme poverty as late as 1950.[6] Nevertheless, prosperity incrementally expanded.[7]

From 1980-2000, over seven hundred million people around the world moved out of the grip of scarcity. Reflecting on this astounding reality, Roser noted,

> Before modern economic growth, the huge majority lived in extreme poverty, and only a tiny elite enjoyed a better living standard. With the onset of industrialization, world poverty started its decline and slowly but steadily a larger share of the world population was lifted out of poverty.[8]

Across the globe, economic revitalization is gaining traction. In the late 1990s, nearly half of China's population lived in extreme poverty. Now this number is less than 1 percent. A similar development is occurring in India—around 88 percent are no longer destitute.[9] Billions across the globe are entering a whole new era of economic opportunity.

---

[6] See Douglas T. Kenrick Ph.D., "Ten Ways the World Is Getting Better: Steven Pinker, Science, Humanism, and Progress," *Psychology Today* (March 2018).

[7] Ibid.

[8] Max Roser, The Short History of Global Living Conditions and Why it Matters that we Know it," *Our World In Data.* https://ourworldindata.org/a-history-of-global-living-conditions-in-5-charts.

[9] See Hans Rosling with Ola Rosling and Anna Rosling Rönnlund, *Factfulness: Ten Reasons We're Wrong About the World—and Why Things Are Better Than You Think* (New York, Flatiron Books, 2018), 53.

Currently, less than 10 percent of the world is gripped by extreme poverty,[10] and by 2030, this figure will likely drop to 3 percent.[11] Berkley notes, that in this trajectory, "misery's billions would be consigned to the annals of history."[12]

Global Poverty Rates 1990-2015

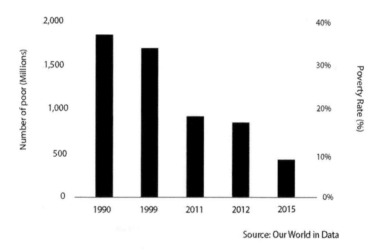

Source: Our World in Data

Reflecting on what is happening in the world, Denning aptly observes,

---

[10] Steve Denning, "Why The World Is Getting Better And Why Hardly Anyone Knows It," *Forbes* (November 2017). Also, see Max Roser, "It's a Cold, Hard Fact: Our World is Becoming a Better Place," *Oxford Martin School* (October 20, 2014).

[11] Nicholas Kristof, "Why 2017 May Be the Best Year Ever," *The New York Times* (January 21, 2017).

[12] Jon Berkley, "Towards the End of Poverty: Nearly 1 Billion People have been Taken out of Extreme Poverty in 20 years," *The Economist* (June 1, 2013).

Amid the flurry of bad news in the media, it's easy to miss how far and how fast we have come. As the media is obsessed with reporting events where things have gone wrong, it is easy to overlook this extraordinary fact: Every single day since 1990, on average, there were 130,000 people fewer in extreme poverty.[13]

The entire globe is experiencing extraordinary financial growth. Market-based economies are expanding exponentially, and millions are experiencing a new standard of living. Reflecting on these developments, Roser notes,

> If we compare the economic prosperity of every region in 2003 with any earlier time, we see that every single region is richer than ever before in its history. Though some regions are more productive than others, every region is doing better than ever before, much better.[14]

Not only is extreme poverty being vanquished, "the world is becoming middle class."[15] Current data suggest that, for the most

---

[13.] Steve Denning, "Why The World Is Getting Better And Why Hardly Anyone Knows It," *Forbes* (November 2017).

[14.] Max Roser, "Economic Growth," Our World in Data, https://ourworldindata.org/economic-growth.

[15.] Steven Pinker, *Enlightenment Now: The Case for Reason, Science, Humanism, and Progress* (New York, Penguin Publishing, 2018), 86.

part, "poor, developing countries" no longer exist as a distinct group.[16]

Hans Rosling observes that most nations are "already inside the box that used to be named 'developed world.'" Together, over 91 percent of humanity now lives in middle and high-income nations. Thus, the notion "of a divided world with a majority stuck in misery and deprivation is an illusion."[17]

Economies that were once weak are now growing exponentially. Poverty is being conquered. Life is becoming better for billions of people around the world.

Famine and Malnourishment

I was chatting with a school official from Lee's Summit, Missouri, about what is happening in the community. Although a majority of the families in this Kansas City suburb have a comfortable income, a percentage still struggles.

I was told that despite the wealth, an astounding number of children in this district go home to an empty refrigerator every night. Teachers sometimes pack up food for the students to take as the last bell rings. I was reminded that hunger shows up in unexpected places.

[16.] Hans Rosling with Ola Rosling and Anna Rosling Rönnlund, *Factfulness: Ten Reasons We're Wrong About the World—and Why Things Are Better Than You Think* (New York, Flatiron Books, 2018), 28.

[17.] Ibid., 27, 32, 33.

A member of my church suggested that if hunger is present in the wealthier neighborhoods of America, it is growing everywhere. He believed that this was an alarming sign of modern society's disintegration.

Warnings about devastating shortages of natural resources—water, electricity, and food—trigger anxiety. I have had several young mothers tell me that they are terrified about not having enough for their children. They have plenty to eat in their refrigerator but have an inexplicable sense of dread.

This type of thought process is not new. Several decades ago Paul Ehrlich warned, "In the 1970s, the world will undergo famines—hundreds of millions of people are going to starve to death."[18] Many academics and activists wrongly believed that America was on the verge of devastating shortages.

In the late 1990s, nervous Americans bought military rations in preparation for the so-called "Y2K bug" that would supposedly disrupt computers and supply chains.[19] They thought that if the grocery store shelves were empty, vacuum-sealed food packages would keep them fed. Nothing out of the ordinary occurred, and those millions of unused military-style rations are now expired.

Over the decades, dire predictions about starvation never materialized. Only small percentages of people have gone without their basic needs being met. In fact, the hunger encountered today is miniscule compared to what was being experienced centuries ago.

[18.] Paul Ehrlich, *The Population Bomb* (New York: Ballantine Books, 1968), 11.

[19.] Scott Kirsner, "Are we Headed for a Global Y2K Crisis?" CNN (March 4, 1999).

Most do not know that malnourishment utterly gripped the world in previous generations. Johan Norberg writes,

> Getting enough energy for the body and the brain to function well is the most basic human need, but historically, it has not been satisfied for most people. Famine was a universal, regular phenomenon.[20]

Pre-modern Europe suffered from famines every few decades.[21] Examining what was occurring, Johan Norberg writes,

> France, one of the wealthiest countries in the world, suffered twenty-six national famines in the eleventh century, two in the twelfth, four in the fourteenth, seven in the fifteenth, thirteen in the sixteenth, eleven in the seventeenth and sixteen in the eighteenth.[22]

Europeans regularly faced crop failures and bouts of severe malnourishment. Vast numbers of the sick and poor died. Hunger gripped every nation.

[20.] Johan Norberg, *Progress: Ten Reasons to Look Forward to the Future* (United Kingdom: One world Publications, 2016), 8.

[21.] Otto Bettmann, *The Good Old Days—They Were Terrible!* (New York: Random House, 1974) 136,

[22.] Johan Norberg, *Progress: Ten Reasons to Look Forward to the Future* (United Kingdom: One world Publications, 2016), 9.

During this period, individuals laboring in workhouses often fought over rotting bones—desiring to suck out the marrow. Pinker notes that

> Desperate peasants would harvest grain before it was ripe, eat grass or human flesh, and pour into cities to beg. Even in good times, many would get the bulk of their calories from bread or gruel, and not many at that.[23]

Over the centuries, famine has also ravaged India, China, and Africa. Unimaginable numbers died in every region of the world. More than seventy million perished in famines triggered by totalitarian regimes. Starvation punctuated Stalin's Holodomor in Ukraine (1932–33), Mao Zedong's Great Leap Forward (1958–61), and Pol Pot's Year Zero (1975-79).[24]

Catastrophes that once gripped millions are disappearing. In the warming glow of the twenty-first century, severe famines no longer affect a majority of the world. Stephen Devereux writes,

> Vulnerability to famine appears to have been virtually eradicated from all regions outside of Africa . . . . The 20th century should go down as

---

[23.] Steven Pinker, *Enlightenment Now: The Case for Reason, Science, Humanism, and Progress* (New York, Penguin Publishing, 2018), 68.

[24.] Ibid., 78.

the last during which tens of millions of people died for lack of access to food.[25]

It is encouraging that large-scale famines are virtually nonexistent, and malnourishment currently affects less than 13 percent of the globe.[26] This truth is astounding when half the world was chronically malnourished decades ago.[27]

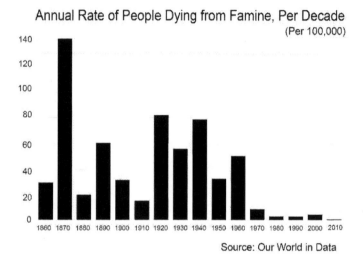

Annual Rate of People Dying from Famine, Per Decade (Per 100,000)

Source: Our World in Data

In the United States, children consume sufficient calories but aren't eating the right kinds of foods. Rather than wasting

---

[25] Stephen Devereux, "Famine in the Twentieth Century," Institute of Development Studies (2000): 3.

[26] "World Hunger Statistics," Food Aid Foundation, (2018), http://www.foodaidfoundation.org/world-hunger-statistics.html

[27] Steven Pinker, *Enlightenment Now: The Case for Reason, Science, Humanism, and Progress* (New York, Penguin Publishing, 2018), 71.

away, they're obese. In many ways, we're wrestling with problems of plenty.[28]

Several decades ago, activists warned that population growth would impoverish the world. They claimed that more mouths to feed would decimate food reserves. But these concerns never materialized.

Despite moving from a global population of three billion in 1960 to almost 7.5 billion in 2018, hunger levels continue to decrease exponentially. Utilizing nearly the same amount of farmland as the mid-twentieth century, food production has increased by 300 percent.[29]

Many don't believe it, but there is currently enough to feed every person on earth. The problem isn't a lack of nutritious dietary options but the ongoing preoccupation with junk food. With so much abundance, how could anyone question the abundance of wealth in this world?

[28.] "Across the globe today there are more people who overeat than who go to bed hungry, a statement that would have seemed fantastical to our great-grandparents, if not to our parents." Gregg Easterbrook, *It's Better Than It Looks: Reasons for Optimism in an Age of Fear* (New York: Public Affairs, 2018), 26.

[29.] Ibid., 76. "In 1961, the world produced 760 million tons of grain; by 2015 the figure was 2.4 billion tons. . . . The 1.1 billion bushels of wheat the United States harvested in 1950 required 84 million acres for cultivation. The 2 billion acres harvested in 2015 required 55 million acres—nearly twice as much yield from one-third fewer acres." Ibid., 8.

Clean Drinking Water

A missionary colleague told me what the poor of Uganda face as they seek to obtain clean drinking water. To cook or bathe, families had to transport containers for miles on foot.[30] When they can access water in this dry environment, it's often filthy and riddled with disease. My friend thought that at one time or another, most of the villagers had become sick after drinking the pollutants.

To acquire clean water, wells have to be dug. Regrettably, their locations were often long distances from villages, and nefarious forces limited access.

My friend paid exorbitant fees to bore new wells in the Ugandan drylands. Because of his love for the people, he did not want them to go without basic needs.

Uganda is not unique in this matter. Around the world, many of the poor have been forced to drink murky water, helpless as cholera, dysentery, and typhoid was transmitted to their families. One of the leading global health concerns has been "microbial contaminated water for drinking and household use."[31] It has been estimated that half a million have died from contaminated water.[32]

[30.] "It has been estimated that collectively African women and children spend forty billion hours per year fetching and carrying water." Johan Norberg, *Progress: Ten Reasons to Look Forward to the Future* (United Kingdom: One world Publications, 2016), 38.

[31.] Ann Lindstrand, Staffan Bergström, Hans Rosling, Birgitta Rubenson, Bo Stenson and Thorild Tylleskär, *Global Health: An Introductory Textbook* (Lund: Studentlitteratur, 2006), 77.

[32.] Various, "Drinking Water," World Health Organization (February 7, 2018). http://www.who.int/news-room/fact-sheets/detail/drinking-water

Fortunately, deficiencies are fading. According to the World Health Organization, 90 percent of the world now has access to clean water.[33] Within a few decades, no family will ever have to drink from a contaminated stream ever again.[34]

Most drinking water is no longer tainted with feces, microbes, or disease. The turbulent rivers are becoming purer. Families in the developing world are being rejuvenated and positioned for a marvelous future.

Global Access To Clean Water

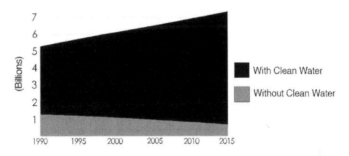

Source: Our World in Data

[33.] Various, "Key Facts from JMP 2015 Report," World Health Organization (2015). http://www.who.int/water_sanitation_health/monitoring/jmp-2015-key-facts/en/

[34.] Ibid.

A More Prosperous World

If one cares to look, signs of economic and infrastructural development are everywhere. Triumphing over poverty, 80 percent of the global population now has most of their basic needs met.[35]

The conclusion of this matter is abundantly clear. The earth is growing more prosperous. Economies are expanding, and families are gaining access to desperately needed resources. The poor are gaining a much better footing.

The town of Hackett, Arkansas, where those young girls tried to get water, still has much to overcome. Nevertheless, residents have opportunities that weren't available in the 1980s. The town is making progress. We can't always see how the world is changing, but it is.

Multitudes are still struggling, but that figure is lower than ever. Poverty's fierce hold on the world has drastically lessened. The claim that the sky is falling is not true. Life in the modern age is significantly better.

[35.] For example, every day, 300,000 people are gaining access to electricity. See Oliver Burkeman, "Is the World Really Better than Ever?" *The Guardian* (July 28, 2017). Also see Hans Rosling with Ola Rosling and Anna Rosling Rönnlund, *Factfulness: Ten Reasons We're Wrong About the World—and Why Things Are Better Than You Think* (New York, Flatiron Books, 2018), 128-129.

6. FIGHT THE POWER
SEXUAL ASSAULT, RACISM, AND INJUSTICE

*"Let justice roll on like a river, righteousness like a
never-failing stream!"*

(AMOS 5:24 NIV)

One of my black friends told me a heartbreaking story. He sent his twelve-year-old daughter into the grocery store to buy a container of chicken for dinner. When she came back to the car, she had the wrong item. So he sent her back in to exchange it.

As she reentered, a white employee accused her of stealing. She tried to explain that she had already purchased the item, and she was merely trying to exchange it, but he wouldn't listen. The unsettling implication was that she could not be trusted because she was black.

Racism, gender bias, and classism have no place in our modern world. It is unconscionable. When injustice raises its ugly head, innocent people get hurt.

A sensible human being cannot ignore the ugliness and pain sparked by injustice. Egregious things have been done to the poor and marginalized. No reasonable person would dispute that truth.

However, is inequality more pronounced in the twenty-first century? Do we see the increased exploitation of the weak? Are gross injustices gaining traction around the world?

Sexual Assault and Gender Inequality

While in the line to vote in the 2016 presidential election, an agitated activist standing near me announced, "Women have it worse than ever before. The time has come to do something about it."[1]

Several appeared to agree with her sentiment. They were convinced that women have been exploited and were unwilling to remain silent about acts of injustice.

Are women genuinely experiencing worsening conditions in the twenty-first century? Are there increasing incidents of bias and sexual assault?

---

[1] Woman next to me in line to vote in the 2016 Presidential election, Lee's Summit, Missouri, Tuesday, November 8, 2016, 5:30 p.m.

Although it feels like life is growing worse, it is not. The modern world is considerably less brutal.

Regarding sexual assault, the ancient world was hideous. Women were considered a "legitimate spoil of war . . . to be enjoyed, monopolized, and disposed of at their pleasure."[2]

In the Roman Coliseum, for example, "naked women were tied to stakes and raped."[3] So-called chivalrous medieval knights regularly abducted women from neighboring kingdoms to gratify their urges.[4] Even soldiers in modern times have continued to rape and pillage war-torn villages.

In ancient societies, women were considered "the property of their fathers and husbands"[5] and were often forced into unwanted relationships. Even as late as nineteenth-century America, the age of sexual consent in many states was nine or ten years of age.[6]

Although sexual assault has been historically under-reported, it's encouraging to see fewer incidents in contemporary records. Pinker observes that in thirty-five years, incidents of sexual assault have

---

[2.] Steven Pinker, *The Better Angels of Our Nature: Why Violence Has Declined* (New York: Penguin Publishing, 2011), 5.

[3.] Ibid., 12.

[4.] Ibid., 18.

[5.] Steven Pinker, *The Better Angels of Our Nature: Why Violence Has Declined* (New York: Penguin Publishing, 2011), 397.

[6.] Harold Eberle, *Victorious Eschatology*, 2nd edition (Yakima, WA: Worldcast Publishing; 2007), 87.

fallen by an astonishing 80 percent, from 250 per 100,000 people over the age of twelve in 1973 to 50 per 100,000 in 2008. In fact, the decline may be even greater than that, because women have almost certainly been more willing to report being raped in recent years, when rape has been recognized as a serious crime, than they were in earlier years, when rape was often hidden and trivialized.[7]

Reports of abuse continue to decrease across the United States. The number of rapes today compared with a generation ago has plummeted. It is hard to imagine, but the number of violations has dropped 80 percent in my lifetime.

Rape and Sexual Victimization, 1995-2010
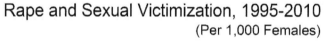
(Per 1,000 Females)

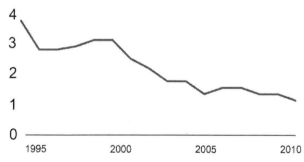

Source: Bureau of Justice Statistics

7. Steven Pinker, *The Better Angels of Our Nature: Why Violence Has Declined* (New York: Penguin Publishing, 2011), 402.

It is horrifying when anyone is victimized, and too many incidents still occur. Nevertheless, it must be acknowledged that social conditions are not as abrasive as they once were.

Misogyny ruled the day in previous generations. For example, in 1900, the only nation where a woman could vote was New Zealand.[8] Reacting to the idea of women participating in politics, *The Oneida Whig Newspaper* asserted the following:

> If our ladies will insist on voting and legislating, where, gentlemen, will be our dinners and our elbows, where our domestic firesides and the holes in our stockings.[9]

Nineteenth-century men were anxious about their laundry and dinner. They worried that their lives would go off the rails if their wives participated in politics. Many males were only concerned with meeting their own needs.

Misogyny remained entrenched. Ivy League colleges didn't accept female students until the 1960s.[10] Throughout most of the twentieth century, women were forbidden from taking out a loan or applying for a credit card.[11] Until a few decades ago, a husband

---

[8.] See Steven Pinker, *Enlightenment Now: The Case for Reason, Science, Humanism, and Progress* (New York, Penguin Publishing, 2018), 222.

[9.] Editor, "Bolting Among the Ladies," *The Oneida Whig* (August 1, 1848).

[10.] Katie McLaughlin, "5 Things Women Couldn't Do in the 1960s," *CNN* (August 25, 2014).

[11.] Steven Pinker, *Enlightenment Now: The Case for Reason, Science, Humanism, and Progress* (New York, Penguin Publishing, 2018), 220.

could legally confine his wife against her will, rape her, and beat her.[12]

Women have been mistreated for eons, but this is fortunately changing. Today most agree that gender bias is indefensible. Society understands that it is unconscionable to celebrate toxic masculinity.

Every human being, regardless of gender, should not only be protected from violence, but they should also have access to educational opportunities.[13] Most agree that no one should be left out.

Although problems persist, society is moving in the right direction. Misogyny is fading in twenty-first century society. Dignity is being quietly restored to a fallen world.

Racism

With riots and social unrest, some believe that racism is at an all-time high in America. One college student was trying to be funny when he declared that tensions between ethnicities hadn't

---

[12.] See Margo Wilson and Martin Daly, "The Man who Mistook his Wife for a Chattel," in J. H. Barkow, L. Cosmides and J. Tooby eds., *The Adapted Mind: Evolutionary Psychology and the Generation of Culture* (New York: Oxford University Press, 1992).

[13.] Fortunately, the proportion of girls in primary school around the world is 90 percent—only two percentage points behind the boys. See Hans Rosling with Ola Rosling and Anna Rosling Rönnlund, *Factfulness: Ten Reasons We're Wrong About the World—and Why Things Are Better Than You Think* (New York, Flatiron Books, 2018), 129.

been this bad since the Civil War.[14] Although intentionally exaggerating, some felt his sentiments were accurate.

Economic and social disparities unfairly impact minorities. When not marginalized or ignored, the urban core is unfairly villainized. Distrust and anger are lying below the surface.

Is bigotry at a higher level than ever before? Are minorities increasingly chastised by the majority culture? Many are convinced that intolerance is growing but historians would disagree. Individuals in the twenty-first century can't image how bigoted and cruel people were in previous eras.

In 1860, racism was blatant in most regions of the United States. Of the 4.4 million people claiming African ancestry, 3.9 million were enslaved.[15] People with different ethnicities were treated like animals—abused and subjected to unconscionable violence. At the time, 25 percent of whites owned a slave. Repugnant behaviors were accepted as the norm.

The ugliness did not go away after slavery was outlawed. In the early 1900s, night raids and lynchings occurred, on average, three times a week.[16] Tar-and-featherings, beatings, and rapes were

---

[14.] Unnamed Kansas University student speaking to me at the Raven bookstore in downtown Lawrence, Kansas on January 28, 2017.

[15.] Stanley L. Engerman, Richard Sutch, and Gavin Wright, "Slavery for Historical Statistics of the United States Millennial Edition," University of California Project on the Historical Statistics of the United States Center for Social and Economic Policy, Policy Studies Institute, University of California, Riverside, March 2003.

[16.] Steven Pinker, *Enlightenment Now: The Case for Reason, Science, Humanism, and Progress* (New York, Penguin Publishing, 2018), 219.

common. The Ku Klux Klan, a bigoted association that President Woodrow Wilson disgracefully praised, brutalized many.[17]

While racism lingers in the United States, it has steadily decreased over time.[18] Most Americans willingly accepted segregation in the mid-twentieth century. At that time, a majority of whites admitted that they would move if a black family became their next-door neighbor. Fortunately, this type of bigotry is becoming more rare.[19] Ellis Close notes,

> Race is less and less an immovable barrier—as evidenced by the small but growing cadre of African-Americans who have risen to the very pinnacle of the worlds of politics and business.[20]

A few indicators are helpful to consider when we discuss the diminishment of bigotry in the United States. One of the most important is the plummeting numbers of hate crimes.[21]

[17.] See Dylan Matthews, "Woodrow Wilson was extremely racist — even by the standards of his time," *Vox* (November 20, 2015). President Franklin Delano Roosevelt's choice for vice president and first Supreme Court nominee were former Ku Klux Klan members. Thad Morgan, "How an Ex-KKK Member Made His Way Onto the U.S. Supreme Court," *History* (October 10, 2018).

[18.] C. K., "Racist Behavior is Declining in America," *Economist* (September 1, 2017).

[19.] See Steven Pinker, *The Better Angels of Our Nature: Why Violence Has Declined* (New York: Penguin Publishing, 2011), 390

[20.] Ellis Close "Meet the New Optimists," *Newsweek* (May 15, 2011).

[21.] Steven Pinker, *Enlightenment Now: The Case for Reason, Science, Humanism, and Progress* (New York, Penguin Publishing, 2018), 219.

In 1994, the FBI documented 6,336 racially motivated crimes. That figure dropped to 3,310 by 2015.[22] Despite what the media portrays, racially motivated violence is decreasing.

Another promising sign is the fewer number of African-Americans killed by police.[23] Although systemic injustice continues in the urban core, the numbers are dropping. Fatal shootings of unarmed black men have diminished over the last three years.[24] Lower levels of brutality are a positive sign of advancement.

An additional marker is declining membership in the Ku Klux Klan. At the organization's peak in the 1920s, it had four million members. Now it has less than three thousand.[25] Fewer people than ever want to be associated with hate groups.

While resentments continue, "straightforward bigotry has declined precipitously."[26] Pockets of racism persist, but intolerance is now distasteful in public discourse. Outside of the glare of the media lights, one will find a far more gracious society.

[22.] Charles Kenny, "The Data Are In: Young People are Increasingly Less Racist than Old People," *Quartz* (May 24, 2017).

[23.] Sendhil Mullainathan, "Police Killings of Blacks: Here Is What the Data Say," *New York Times* (October 16, 2015).

[24.] John Sullivan, Julie Tate, and Jennifer Jenkins, "Fatal Police Shootings of Unarmed People have Significantly Declined, Experts Say," *Washington Post* (May 7, 2018).

[25.] Megan Trimble, "KKK Groups Still Active in These States in 2017," *U.S. News and World Reports* (August 14, 2017).

[26.] Sheri Berman, "Why Identity Politics Benefits the Right More than the Left," *The Guardian* (July 14, 2018).

Although leaders in minority communities continue to point out inequalities, some are willing to acknowledge progress. Larry Elder, a black attorney, pointed out,

> America is more inclusive and just than at any point in her history. When one considers the staggering diversity and continued prosperity of the American people, racism approaches near insignificance.[27]

Thomas Sowell, a distinguished black economist, also weighed in on this subject, suggesting that racism continues because of the scourge of partisan politics. He writes,

> Racism is not dead, but it is on life support—kept alive by politicians, race hustlers and people who get a sense of superiority by denouncing others as "racists."[28]

Sadly some power brokers try to gain the upper hand by widening the racial divide. They pit one ethnicity against another. Fortunately most people see through this ruse. Battling an atmosphere of media-infused suspicion, many want to contend for a culture of honor. They want to find a way for diverse ethnicities to find a place of agreement and respect.

[27.] Larry Elder, *What's Race Got to Do with It?: Why It's Time to Stop the Stupidest Argument in America* (New York: St. Martin's Press, 2009), 2.

[28.] Thomas Sowell, "Random Thoughts," *Jewish World Review* (February 2, 2016).

In fact, a trajectory toward racial equality is evident around the world.[29] Between 1950 and 2003, the proportion of countries with policies that discriminated against minorities fell from 44 percent to 19 percent. Many of these nations reversed laws and instituted new policies that protect the marginalized.[30]

The world is changing for the better. Researchers from *The Economist* recently pointed out that "inequality of life outcomes is declining both across and within countries."[31] Discrimination is rapidly fading in the modern world.

Fewer people than ever want to be associated with injustice. The world is moving in the right direction. Society is drastically less racist than it has ever been in history.

Abortion

Some vehemently reject the notion of progress. For these people, sin and enduring social problems undercut any claims of advancement. An agitated truck driver from Springfield, Missouri, once remarked to me,

---

[29.] While Slavery existed in almost all nations as late as 1800, it is now formally banned everywhere.

[30.] Victor Asal and Amy Pate, "The Decline of Ethnic Political Discrimination, 1950-2003," in *Peace and Conflict 2005: A Global Survey of Armed Conflicts, Self-Determination Movements, and Democracy*, edited by Monty G. Marshall, Ted Robert Gurr (University of Maryland: Center for International Development, 2005).

[31.] The Data Team, "Life in Developing Countries Continues to Improve," *The Economist* (September 14, 2018).

How can you say that society is moving forward when millions of babies are aborted? Whenever increasing numbers of children are dying, it is an indictment of our depraved culture. You are a fool to believe that the world is getting better.[32]

I understood his anger. The inexplicable number of babies killed over the last generation is a travesty. Ignoring this injustice is inexcusable.

But he mistakenly believed that abortions were only instituted after Roe v. Wade in 1973.[33] He was unaware it had been an ongoing practice for centuries.

As appalling as abortion statistics are in the twenty-first century, a disturbing number of babies were also taken in previous generations. Past and present rates of termination aren't as dissimilar as many believe.

Beginning in the eighteenth century, American women who wanted to end pregnancies utilized herbal concoctions and toxic drugs.[34] By the 1800s, an estimated 20 percent of pregnancies were aborted annually. At that time, Michigan had the highest rate—34 percent. Throughout the nineteenth century, as many as two million abortions were performed every year.[35]

[32.] An unnamed truck driver spoke to me at the Redeemed Books and Music store in Springfield, Missouri on June 28, 2013.

[33.] Roe v. Wade, 410 U.S. 113 (1973) is a Supreme Court decision on the issue of the constitutionality of laws that criminalized or restricted access to abortions.

[34.] Katha Pollitt, "Abortion in American History," *The Atlantic* (May 1997).

[35.] Ibid.

The fact that so many pregnancies were terminated in previous eras is unfathomable. But these are not the kinds of stories recounted in beloved family histories.

Keep in mind that although the lives of 744,600 babies were cut short the first year abortion was legalized,[36] a comparable 800,000 were terminated in the early twentieth century.[37] This abysmally high annual rate is one of the unspoken horrors of America's past.

Many are convinced that more infants are being aborted in the twenty-first century. Among segments of the American population, this is considered an unassailable truth. But data provides a different viewpoint. Ariana Eunjung Cha of *The Washington Post* points out,

> In the years immediately after abortion was legalized nationwide in 1973, the number of legal abortions rose dramatically, reaching its peak in the 1980s. Abortions then began dropping at a slow rate until around 2006 to 2008, when they increased slightly, followed by even greater decreases in recent years.[38]

[36.] Randall K. O'Bannon, Ph.D., "Out of the Long Dark Night: Abortion Statistics and Trends over the Past Thirty Years," *National Right To Life* (2003).

[37.] Matt Ford, "What Caused the Great Crime Decline in the U.S.?" *The Atlantic* (April 15, 2016)

[38.] Ariana Eunjung Cha, "Number of Abortions in U.S. hit Historic Low in 2015, the most recent year for which data is available," *Washington Post* (Wednesday, November 21, 2018).

Not only are fewer abortions performed,[39] but American health officials are reporting record lows.[40] Tara C. Jatlaoui, from the Center for Disease Control, acknowledges, "The number, rate, and ratio of reported abortions have declined across all race/ethnicity groups."[41] Chuck Donovan, president of the Charlotte Lozier Institute, points out that the decline is "sharp and consistent . . . half of what it was in 1980."[42] There are indications of the rate dropping even more in the years ahead.[43] Cha reiterates, "Fewer U.S. women are having abortions than at any time since Roe v. Wade."[44]

Within the blinding fog of despair, there are promising signs of hope. Fewer pregnancies are being terminated and innocent babies are being given a chance at life. Abortion's downward trend is an indication of wonderful advancements in our

---

[39] Editor, "Abortion Above the Law (In a Good Way)," *Christianity Today* 59:7 (September 2015): 16. The abortion rate was 11.8 abortions per 1,000 women ages 15-44 in 2015, compared with 12.1 in 2014 and 15.9 in 2006.

[40] Ibid.

[41] Tara C. Jatlaoui, from the CDC's division of reproductive health quoted in Ariana Eunjung Cha, "Number of abortions in U.S. hit historic low in 2015, the most recent year for which data is available," *Washington Post* (Wednesday, November 21, 2018).

[42] Chuck Donovan quoted in Ariana Eunjung Cha, "Number of abortions in U.S. hit historic low in 2015, the most recent year for which data is available," *Washington Post* (Wednesday, November 21, 2018).

[43] Various, "CDCs Abortion Surveillance System FAQs, Centers For Disease Control," *Center For Disease Control*, (2015). https://www.cdc.gov/reproductivehealth/data_stats/Abortion.html.

[44] Ariana Eunjung Cha, "Number of abortions in U.S. hit historic low in 2015, the most recent year for which data is available," *Washington Post* (Wednesday, November 21, 2018).

world. Justice is finally gaining a foothold in the twenty-first century.

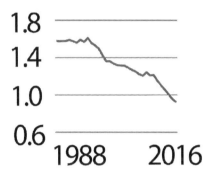

Total Number of U.S. Abortions in Millions

Source: Alan Guttmacher Institute

Beauty Should Never Be Distorted

When I share positive changes that are happening, some become angry with me. They believe that I'm making light of the offence of injustice. One young woman recently told me, "You're discounting the wretchedness and pain of inequality."[45]

I don't want to give the impression that all is right. Sometimes the strong take advantage of the weak. Sexual assault,

---

[45.] This was a conversation with young woman at a Starbucks coffee shop in Lee's Summit, Missouri in the fall of 2017.

racism, and abortion still occur in our world, bringing shame upon everyone.

When I talked with my friend about how they treated his daughter at the grocery store, I wanted to let him know how sorry I was. No one should have to experience that level of humiliation. He thanked me and told me that he appreciated my concern for his family.

Although the world is far from perfect, I am grateful that injustice isn't as dominant as it once was. For the most part, prejudice is abhorred, and tolerance demanded. Many in our society are infuriated when people distort heaven's beautiful design.

Not all live up to their God-ordained identity, but love remains a powerful motivator. Hearts are changing. Today is considerably better than yesterday. Inequality is vanishing as the value for human dignity is reinvigorating the nations.

7. IN THE GAPS BETWEEN THE STORIES
WHY THE WORLD IS GETTING BETTER

"For the grace of God has been revealed, bringing
salvation to all people."

(TITUS 2:11 NLT)

A few years ago, I had an engaging discussion with a college professor about the future of the world. We were both examining the latest releases at a Barnes and Noble bookstore and struck up a conversation.

I told him about some of the positive developments that I had discovered during my studies. The facts of fewer wars and increasing economic opportunity seized his attention. He was delighted to hear that magnificent things were taking place in the world.

As the conversation continued, he asked me why I thought this was occurring. He wanted to know the basis for these thrilling changes.

I told him that I thought that the explanations were obvious. Most nations have become better at harnessing science, education, and sound economic policy. Mutually beneficial trade agreements, conscientious government, and technological advances are also fueling this progress.

Although agreeing, he prodded me. With a coy look on his face, he asked, "Don't you think that there is something more? It's hard to believe that 'soulless science' is the real reason for fewer wars." It was almost as if we were swapping roles. I sounded like an academic, and he approached me like a pastor.

I acknowledged that something more was transpiring. The positive developments taking place are about more than mechanisms. Our attention should naturally turn to questions about worldview. Technology is merely an actualization of our value systems. Ideals are hardwired into the worlds that we build.

I paused for a moment and told him that Christianity might be the reason that so much is changing. Followers of Jesus are increasing and likely bearing fruit in places all over the world.

I explained that a biblically rooted faith is generous and concerned for the poor. It has a value system that concentrates on the importance of justice. It is not selfish or motivated by violence.

The professor lit up, and a smile crossed his face. I realized that he shared my outlook. For us, Christianity is part of what is enabling beauty and goodness to take root in this world.

Secularism's Spector

Not everyone agrees that Christians are positive change agents. Some think that believers are impeding global progress.[1] Most academics see religion as an anachronism. They believe that a world devoid of war, poverty, and inequality is irreligious.

For centuries, Western intellectuals have emphasized "the inevitability of a worldwide triumph of secularization."[2] They are convinced religion will be displaced by reason.

For many atheists, "secularization is an unshakable matter of faith."[3] Marx, Nietzsche, and Freud argued that religion "would surely disappear by the 21st-century, or at least its role in human society would diminish."[4]

A sociologist writing in *The New York Times* in 1968 made a similar assertion. He said that by the twenty-first century,

---

[1] Those that would veer away from accepting Christian influence include: Stephen Pinker, Hans Rosling, Max Roser, Gregg Easterbrook, Johan Norberg, and Matt Ridley. Each of these gifted analysts are referenced throughout this book.

[2] Rodney Stark, *Triumph Of Faith: Why The World Is More Religious Than Ever* (Intercollegiate Studies Institute, 2015), 54-55.

[3] Ibid., 2.

[4] Donald E. Miller, "Introduction: Pentecostalism As A Global Phenomenon," *Spirit and Power: The Growth and Global Impact of Pentecostalism*, eds., Donald E, Miller, Kimon H. Sargeant, and Richard Flory (New York, Oxford University Press, 2013), 10.

Christians were "likely to be found only in small sects, huddled together to resist a worldwide secular culture."[5]

Many intellectuals love to contemplate religion's decline in America and Europe.[6] They are convinced that it is only a matter of time before we are residing in a post-Christian era.

I assumed that the professor at Barnes and Noble was opposed to religion. I don't know if it was his demeanor or something else, but he gave off the vibe of a secularist. So I was pleasantly surprised to discover that he was also a Christ-follower.

To be honest, many of the professionals that I've engaged over the years reject secularism. Even those not attending church services were not opposed to the intersection of religion in our world. The multitudes still seem intrigued by God.

Sometimes our shared narratives turn out to be distorted. Rodney Stark, a sociologist from Baylor University, points out that much of the talk about secularization is "unfounded nonsense."[7] The twenty-first century world is more religious than ever.

Across the globe, 80 percent belong to some form of organized religion,[8] and less than 5 percent are atheist.[9] The so-

---

[5.] Peter Berger, "A Bleak Outlook Is Seen for Religion," *New York Times* (April 25, 1968), 3.

[6.] Ibid., 1.

[7.] Rodney Stark, *Triumph Of Faith: Why The World Is More Religious Than Ever* (Intercollegiate Studies Institute, 2015), 10.

[8.] This number would obviously include adherents of Christianity, Islam, Judaism, Hinduism, and other faith traditions.

[9.] Rodney Stark, *Triumph Of Faith: Why The World Is More Religious Than Ever* (Intercollegiate Studies Institute, 2015), 1.

called "decline of faith" in the modern era "is merely wishful thinking and entirely at odds with reliable data."[10]

Stark points out that

> Secularists have been predicting the imminent demise of religion for centuries. They have always been wrong— and their claims today are no different. It is their unshakeable faith in secularization that may be the most "irrational" of all beliefs.[11]

For the most part, individuals are blind to the contributions Christians are making to contemporary society. The church is more pivotal to modern life than many imagine.

Moving Beyond a Caricature

I once interacted with an atheist who liked to ridicule Christians. To him, churchgoers were merely uneducated, gun fanatics who squelch political discourse. He was an open-minded progressive but behaved like a bigot.

Many believe this crude caricature of Christianity. Unfamiliar with the diversity of this burgeoning global religion, they conflate biblical faith with right-wing politics.

[10.] Ibid., 2.

[11.] Ibid., 212.

Most don't realize that Christianity plays a vital role in the modern world, contributing "to the emergence of concepts such as freedom of conscience, tolerance, and the separation of powers."[12]

Spanning the globe, Christian institutions assist in "health care, education, social support, finding marriage partners, assisting with overseas travel, business, and finding jobs."[13]

A panelist, speaking to the Council on Foreign Relations in Washington D.C., pointed out that Christian communities are often marked by

> internalized self-discipline, respect for the law as an objective reflection of God's righteousness, and altruistic care for those who are least able to care for themselves.[14]

My atheist acquaintance didn't comprehend this, but the church addresses the precariousness of life. Christianity often wrestles with modernity's spiritual deficiencies and provides meaning.

---

[12] R. G., "Why is Protestantism Flourishing in the Developing World?" *The Economist* (November 9, 2017).

[13] Rosalind I.J. Hackett quoted in "Christianity Growing Fast in Parts of Latin America, Africa, Asia," *Billings Gazette* (May 10, 2002).

[14] Mark Noll, "Faith and Conflict: The Global Rise of Christianity," Council on Foreign Relations and Pew Research Center (March 2, 2005).

Expanding Economics

Against the backdrop of modernization and fluctuating market economies, Christianity is reshaping global business practices[15] and creating an environment for developing economies.[16]

Mao Zedong, a Communist revolutionary, decimated all religious expressions in China in 1949. In doing so, he created a spiritual vacuum. As this collectivist regime faced instability, it grasped for more than ideology. Peering beyond the hollowness of Communism, many desired "a new moral compass."[17]

A Chinese scholar recounted the following to a group of American researchers:

> In the past twenty years, we have realized that the heart of your culture is your religion: Christianity. That is why the West is so powerful. The Christian moral foundation of social and cultural life was what made possible the emergence of capitalism

---

[15.] See Bill Murphy, "China, Officially Atheist, Could have more Christians than the U.S. by 2030," *Houston Chronicle* (February 24, 2018).

[16.] See Jerry Bowyer, "Is Religion An Essential Driver Of Economic Growth?" *Forbes* (May 29, 2013).

[17.] Mark Noll, "Faith and Conflict: The Global Rise of Christianity," Council on Foreign Relations and Pew Research Center (March 2, 2005).

and then the transition to democratic politics. We don't have any doubts about this.[18]

The Chinese wanted not only an ethical framework for business, but also a sense of purpose. As soon as capitalism took root, Christianity began to grow.[19] Soon the church gained influence in every corner of the People's Republic.

Whether bolstering impoverished conditions or stabilizing chaotic growth, Christianity advances when it's "embraced as a point of stability in an economically insecure world."[20] Mark Noll suggests,

> In the great favelas and barrios of Latin America and the Philippines, as well as the teeming cities of Africa, Christian faith thrives among people whose economic existence is precarious.[21]

The church is not merely providing dignity for the poor. It champions honesty, punctuality, and hard work, values that sustain market economies.[22] Where there are large-scale economic reforms

---

[18.] A scholar from the Chinese Academy of Social Sciences in Beijing quoted in David Aikman, *Jesus in Beijing: How Christianity Is Transforming China and Changing the Global Balance of Power* (Washington, DC: Regnery, 2003), 5.

[19.] Fenggang Yang quoted in Bill Murphy, "China, Officially Atheist, Could have More Christians than the U.S. by 2030," *Houston Chronicle* (February 24, 2018).

[20.] Mark Noll, "Faith and Conflict: The Global Rise of Christianity," Council on Foreign Relations and Pew Research Center (March 2, 2005).

[21.] Ibid.

[22.] Michael Nazir-Ali, "Faith and Conflict: The Global Rise of Christianity," Council on Foreign Relations and Pew Research Center (March 2, 2005).

and urban migration, one will find Christianity. Its cultural malleability "makes it suitable to populations on the move, seeking new social identities and communities."[23]

Championing Human Dignity

Not all critics are aware that Christianity is concerned with human dignity. They don't know that the Bible asserts that everyone—regardless of social standing—is fashioned in God's image.[24] All human beings are valuable in God's kingdom and are worthy of affection.

Where justice emerges, there will always be an increasing number of Christians. For example, thousands are coming to faith in Nepal, escaping the bonds of an entrenched caste system.[25] In this part of the world, the dregs of society are discovering God's love.

Throughout Africa, multitudes are embracing the church, not only because of its stand on equality[26] but also because it challenges "cultural beliefs that marginalize women."[27]

[23.] R. G., "Why is Protestantism Flourishing in the Developing World?" *The Economist* (November 9, 2017).

[24.] See Genesis 1:26a: "Then God said, 'Let us make human beings in our image, to be like us.'"

[25.] Agence France-Presse, "How Christianity is Spreading in Nepal Despite Conversion Ban," *South China Morning Post* (December 23, 2017).

[26.] Rodney Stark, *Triumph Of Faith: Why The World Is More Religious Than Ever* (Intercollegiate Studies Institute, 2015), 121.

[27.] Sylvia Bawa, "Christianity, Tradition, and Gender Inequality in Postcolonial Ghana," *African Geographical Review* (February 2017): 1-16.

In Latin America, believers feverously advocate for the family, confronting infidelity, substance abuse, and domestic violence. Michael Nazir-Ali said the Christians

> are family friendly. They are hostile to male machismo culture, which is out in the streets and on the soccer fields and engages in, you know, weekend binge drinking and all those sorts of things. So it is for the building up of the family.[28]

Across the globe, Christians encircle the marginalized. In the midst of confusion and fear, believers are building life-affirming communities. A faith that's restoring human dignity captures the gaze of millions.

Transforming Health

Detractors suggest that Christianity is too heavenly minded to be any earthly good. In this thinking, mysticism makes one oblivious to the needs of others. This is a distorted perspective.

From the beginning, Christendom has emphasized caring for the sick.[29] In many parts of the world, inadequate medical services plague the poor. Christians naturally want to fill in the gap.

[28.] Michael Nazir-Ali, "Faith and Conflict: The Global Rise of Christianity," Council on Foreign Relations and Pew Research Center (March 2, 2005).

[29.] See J.D. King, *Regeneration: A Complete History of Healing in the Christian Church* (Lees Summit, Missouri: Christos Publishing, 2017).

As believers comfort the diseased, they offer words of encouragement and prayer. Meaningful rituals form. For many, this becomes a compelling reason to be a part of the Christian community.

In South Africa, the church is growing because it addresses healing within their cultural context. From the perspective of Africans, recuperative practices should address "more than just a body ailment, but the totality of a person."[30]

Agence France-Presse recounts the story of Rika Tamang, a Nepalese man who converted to Christianity after his sick mother could not pay for animal sacrifices required by a shaman. Followers of Jesus addressed needs and invited the Tamang family to be a part of their community.[31]

Conversion testimonies that Donald Miller encountered in China, the Philippines, and other parts of Asia were based on recuperative help received from the church.[32] Christianity's ability to help counteract the rigors of disease is one of the most compelling catalysts for evangelism in the twenty-first century.

[30.] James Kenokeno Mashabela, "Healing in a Cultural Context: The Role of Healing as a Defining Character in the Growth and Popular Faith of the Zion Christian Church," Diss. University of South Africa, 2017, 1.

[31.] See Michael Nazir-Ali, "Faith and Conflict: The Global Rise of Christianity," Council on Foreign Relations and Pew Research Center (March 2, 2005).

[32.] Donald E. Miller, "Introduction: Pentecostalism As A Global Phenomenon," in *Spirit and Power: The Growth and Global Impact of Pentecostalism*, eds., Donald E, Miller, Kimon H. Sargeant, and Richard Flory (New York, Oxford University Press, 2013), 10.

Answering Existential Questions

Western analysts tend to write off the church, labeling it a relic of a bygone era. Deeming religion a moralistic annoyance, they find little value in biblical teaching.

Fortunately, I've encountered individuals with a different outlook. They believe that Christianity can provide viable answers to many of life's most difficult questions.

Religious revival and societal betterment are often closely interrelated. Rodney Stark asserted, "Only religion provides credible and satisfactory answers to the great existential questions."[33]

Could it even be possible that Christianity is responsible for the improving state of society? At the outset, it might seem improbable if not impossible. But what if I told you there was substantial evidence that the church is impacting the world?

[33.] Rodney Stark, *Triumph Of Faith: Why The World Is More Religious Than Ever* (Intercollegiate Studies Institute, 2015), 212.

SECTION TWO

"It's like in the great stories Mr. Frodo, the ones that really mattered. Full of darkness and danger they were, and sometimes you didn't want to know the end because how could the end be happy? How could the world go back to the way it was when so much bad had happened? But in the end it's only a passing thing this shadow, even darkness must pass. A new day will come, and when the sun shines, it'll shine out the clearer."

—Samwise Gamgee,
The Lord of the Rings, The Two Towers

8. CONTINUOUS AS THE STARS THAT SHINE
CHRISTIANITY'S INEXPLICABLE WONDER

"The kingdom of heaven is like yeast that a woman
mixed into a large amount of flour until the yeast
worked its way through all the dough."

(MATTHEW 13:33 NIV)

A student from the Revival Training Center where I instruct had been reading articles and was worried about Christianity's future. The blogs and magazines that he perused told him that Christianity had lost its footing and was becoming obsolete.

Over a cup of coffee, I explained that the articles were missing much of what was happening in the world. While Europe and the United States might be experiencing setbacks, Christianity is exploding in other parts of the globe. I explained that he had nothing to worry about.

Almost two centuries ago, Jesus told his followers, "I will build my church, and all the powers of hell will not conquer it" (Matthew 16:18b NLT). We cannot dismiss this declaration. The church is not diminishing and has never been in retreat. Faith is prevailing in our world.

The Overcoming Church

I've had conversations with missiologists and researchers. I've learned that Christianity is a global phenomenon. Throughout history, multitudes have identified with Jesus. This has been particularly evident over the last few generations. In recent eras, the "Christian penetration of local cultures has accelerated as never before."[1]

During the previous century, the church has nearly quadrupled—600 million in 1910 to 2.3 billion in 2011.[2] Remarkably, over a third of the earth currently identifies with Jesus.

Interacting with some of the statistical data, George Weigel recounted, "There will be, by mid-2011, 2,306,609,000

---

[1] Mark Noll, "Faith and Conflict: The Global Rise of Christianity," Council on Foreign Relations and Pew Research Center (March 2, 2005).

[2] Some set the figure as high as 3.2 billion, but this is contested—with many researchers offering lower numbers. Most estimate 2.2 billion Christians. Rodney Stark, *Triumph Of Faith: Why The World Is More Religious Than Ever* (Intercollegiate Studies Institute, 2015), 12.

Christians of all kinds in the world, representing 33 percent of the world population."[3]

This staggering figure represents an unprecedented realignment. Christianity has been gaining a significant foothold. Extrapolating data from the Statistics Task Force of the Lausanne Committee for World Evangelism, we observe the following:

> At AD 100, 1/360th of the world population was Christian. By AD 1000, 1/220th of the world population was Christian. By 1500, the percentage of Christians rose to 1/69th of the worldwide population. By 1900, with a world population of slightly over one billion, Christianity had risen to 1/27th of the population. By 1990, the percentage of Christians rose to 1/7th of the worldwide population. As was stated previously, it is now estimated that there are seven billion people on planet Earth and that a full one-third of them (one out of every three people worldwide) are followers of Jesus![4]

The growth isn't slowing. Pew Research Center surmises that within decades, the global Christian population will surpass

---

[3.] George Weigel, "Christian Number-Crunching Reveals Impressive Growth," *Catholic Education Resource Center* (February 9, 2011).

[4.] "The 1990 Report of the Statistics Task Force of the Lausanne Committee for World Evangelism," Wheaton College, https://www2.wheaton.edu/bgc/archives/guides/046.html

three billion. Other analysts believe that the numbers might increase even more. Most do not realize that the church is the most dominant force on the planet.

Global Christian Expansion

■ Christian growth slower than population growth
■ Christian growth faster than population growth

Source: Operation World

Will Islam Surpass Christianity?

Not everyone acknowledges Christianity's burgeoning expansion. A Baptist pastor from Independence, Missouri, cautioned that the church is declining while Islam is on the rise.

Citing *The Clash of Civilizations* by Samuel Huntington, he ominously declared, "in the long run, Muhammad wins out."[5]

I replied that Huntington and other like-minded analysts are mistaken. The church is not losing ground to Islam. In fact, Christian conversions have been outpacing Muslim growth for decades. According to Bruce Milne, Protestant growth was three times global population changes and twice that of Islam from 1960-2000.[6] While shortsighted analysts have predicted the demise of Christianity for generations, their ominous predictions have continued to be wrong.

Denouncing the inevitability of Islam's dominance, Rodney Stark noted the following:

> As recently as April 2015, the Pew Research Center declared that Muslims will soon overtake Christians by way of superior fertility. They won't . . . . Islam generates very little growth through conversions, while Christianity enjoys a substantial conversion rate, especially in nations located in what my colleague Philip Jenkins describes as the "global south"—Asia, Sub-Saharan Africa, and Latin America. And these conversions do not include the millions of converts being gained in

---

[5] Samuel Huntington, *The Clash of Civilizations and the Remaking of World Order* (New York: Simon & Schuster, 1998) 65. I had this conversation in a Lifeway Bookstore in Olathe, Kansas in the summer of 2017.

[6] Bruce Milne, *Know the Truth: A Handbook of Christian Belief* (Downer's Grove: InterVarsity Press, 2010), 332.

China. Thus, current growth trends project an increasingly Christian world.[7]

In years past, Islamic growth occurred because of high birth rates. Muslim women tend to have a number of children. Nevertheless, this disparity is ending.[8] In his research, Hans Rosling discovered that there's "no major difference between the birth rates."[9] Other analysts suggest that differences remain, but the gap is closing. The Pew Research Center, for example, writes,

> The gap in fertility between the Christian and Muslim-dominated nations fell from 67% in 1990 to 17% in 2010. If the trend continues, the Muslim and Christian fertility rates will converge in around 2050.[10]

We should consider other dynamics when contrasting Islam and Christianity. While Muslims are concentrated in the Middle East, there's not a single region "without significant

---

[7.] Rodney Stark, *Triumph Of Faith: Why The World Is More Religious Than Ever* (Intercollegiate Studies Institute, 2015), 19.

[8.] Ibid.

[9.] "Today, Muslim women have on average 3.1 children. Christian women have 2.7." Hans Rosling with Ola Rosling and Anna Rosling Rönnlund, *Factfulness: Ten Reasons We're Wrong About the World—and Why Things Are Better Than You Think* (New York, Flatiron Books, 2018), 176.

[10.] Various, "The Future of World Religions: Population Growth Projections, 2010-2050," Pew Research Center (April 2, 2015).

numbers of Christians."[11] Followers of Jesus are "so far-flung and geographically widespread," that "no single continent or region can indisputably claim to be the center of global Christianity."[12] Stark observes that

> Christianity is not only the largest religion in the world; it also is the least regionalized . . . . There are only trivial numbers of Muslims in the Western Hemisphere and East Asia."[13]

Other distinctions are obvious. Islam demands allegiance to the Arabic language and ancient Middle Eastern culture. Christians, in contrast, encourage adherents to read the Bible in their own languages. The church is not shackled to any ethnicity or cultural expression.

Perhaps nowhere is the distinction between these religious traditions more evident than in modes of conversion. Where Islam has advanced through childbirth and coercion, healing and interpersonal engagement are fueling Christian growth. Make no mistake about it; the church is globally expansive and showing no signs of letting up.[14]

[11.] Rodney Stark, *Triumph Of Faith: Why The World Is More Religious Than Ever* (Intercollegiate Studies Institute, 2015), 16.

[12.] Various, "Global Christianity – A Report on the Size and Distribution of the World's Christian Population," Pew Research Center (December 19, 2011).

[13.] Rodney Stark, *Triumph Of Faith: Why The World Is More Religious Than Ever* (Intercollegiate Studies Institute, 2015), 16.

[14.] See Various, "Global Statistics, 2005-2010," *Operation World*. http://www.operationworld.org/.

False Conversions?

I was discussing Christianity and the condition of the world with a colleague. He was open to what I was sharing but ultimately disagreed with my conclusions. He remarked, "The world might be better in a socio-economic sense, but it's not improving morally or spiritually."[15]

He felt that I was making too much of my data points. With a sense of consternation, he asked, "How could society be improving if so many terrible things are being done in our nation?"

I told him that while some believe that American culture has coarsened,[16] it would be wrong to suggest that depravity has skyrocketed. America had plenty of problems, but isn't becoming worse. Rather than losing ground, Christians are advancing in a number of different ways.

He said, "J.D., the revival that you claim is happening isn't genuine. Come on, you don't believe that those escalating figures represent real conversions, do you? If that many people were devoted to Jesus, surely we would hear something about it."

I understood his thought process. It's easy to imagine that one has a finger on the pulse. Substantial events taking place outside one's field of vision seems impossible. Nevertheless, it's not always wise to generalize.

[15.] This was a conversation that I had with Pentecostal pastor from Kansas City, Missouri.

[16.] Charles Colson suggested this in Alex McFarland, "Rampant Immorality Threatens U.S.'s Future," *The Charlotte Observer* (April 9, 2016).

Outside of the distracted gaze of America, millions of people are earnestly embracing Christianity. What these new converts are encountering shouldn't be dismissed. God is up to astounding things.

Reflecting on the viability of conversions in the developing world, Rodney Stark noted the following:

> Some might argue that the tens of millions of new Christians aren't really more religious than they were a century ago, that all they have done is abandoned their tribal religions for Christianity. But the fact is that the Christians of southern Africa pursue their new faith with far greater intensity than they did their tribal religions. For one thing, all across the region church attendance rates are significantly higher than anywhere else.[17]

The notion that the spiritual awakening in Africa, Asia, and Latin America is a sham is unnerving. It not only belittles the work of the Spirit, but it also smacks of racism. Are revivals only valid if they emerge from white evangelicals in the United States?

Many of the harshest critics are under the impression that holiness and devotion are absent from the global Christian community. They forget that many coming into the church are

---

[17.] Rodney Stark, *Triumph Of Faith: Why The World Is More Religious Than Ever* (Intercollegiate Studies Institute, 2015), 125.

doing so in the face of severe persecution. Where faith is growing the most is where people are killed for embracing it.

Mohamed-Christophe Bilek, a beleaguered former Muslim from Northern Africa, noted the following:

> For those of us who have come out of Islam, following Christ has consequences . . . . it requires a break with the past, with family, with community, and with moral and spiritual certitudes. It's much easier to remain a Muslim, believe me![18]

Ignorant detractors question the escalating numbers. They don't realize that the most dynamic Christian growth is taking place in environments historically opposed to missionaries. Violent and antagonistic locales—China, Northern Africa, India, and Venezuela—are experiencing an unprecedented outpouring of the Holy Spirit.

Genuine revival is erupting across the globe. Millions of people are entering the kingdom of God. These devoted men and women long to see the goodness of Jesus manifest in this world.

[18.] Mohamed-Christophe Bilek quoted in Bassam Michael Madany, "Muslims Converting To Christ: A Sign of the Times," *Academia.edu* (November 26, 2018).

9. I BLESS THE RAINS DOWN IN AFRICA
CHRISTIANITY'S EXPANSION IN AFRICA

*"The LORD has proclaimed His salvation and
revealed His righteousness to the nations."*

(PSALM 98:2 NIV)

I have friends who serve as missionaries in Africa. In addition to
caring for orphans and sharing scripture, they reflect the love of
Jesus in a myriad of ways. I enjoy hearing their amazing accounts
of breakthrough.

What has been transpiring across the continent of Africa
over the last century is awe-inspiring. In 1900, nearly every person

embraced Islam or tribal religions.[1] Since that time, Christianity
has moved from the margins to the center of African life. The
expansion of the Christian church across the continent is an
astonishing phenomenon.[2]

George Weigel suggests that

> Africa has been the most stunning area of Christian
> growth over the past century. There were 8.7
> million African Christians in 1900 (primarily in
> Egypt, Ethiopia, and South Africa); there are 475
> million African Christians today, and their
> numbers are projected to reach 670 million by
> 2025.[3]

Weigel's observations are backed by the analysis of the Pew
Research Center. Their data also point to incredible changes. They
report that

> The share of the population that is Christian in
> sub-Saharan Africa climbed from 9 percent in 1910

---

[1] Rodney Stark, *Triumph Of Faith: Why The World Is More Religious Than Ever* (Intercollegiate Studies Institute, 2015), 107.

[2] See Diarmaid MacCulloch, *Christianity: The First Three Thousand Years* (New York: Viking, 2009), 965.

[3] George Weigel, "Christian Number-Crunching Reveals Impressive Growth," *Catholic Education Resource Center* (February 9, 2011).

to 63 percent in 2010, or from 8.5 million to 516 million during that time.[4]

Likewise, Candy Brown of Indiana University couldn't disregard the "striking growth of Christianity in Africa." Her studies suggest that the church has moved from 5 to 48 percent of the continent, an unprecedented expansion.[5]

Sub-Sahara Africa

Across Sub-Sahara Africa, there is evidence of monumental shifts. For example, missionaries Heidi and Roland Baker, with over 2,700 church plants, have made a far-reaching impact in Mozambique.

Pemba, the province that the Bakers operate in, was deemed 99 percent Muslim before their arrival. Fifteen years later, those figures are remarkably different. Kelly Head writes,

> The Bakers are now based full-time in Pemba, Mozambique, in an area where Heidi says was once called a "graveyard to missionaries." But recently the government announced that it's no longer a

---

[4] Pew Research Report, "Global Christianity – A Report on the Size and Distribution of the World's Christian Population" (December 19, 2011).

[5] Candy Brown quoted in Sunday Oguntola and Ruth Moon, "Antibodies or The Almighty? Ebola Outbreak Highlights African Views About God's Healing Power," *Christianity Today* 58:9 (November 2014), 19.

Muslim providence; now it's a Christian providence.[6]

Other astounding accounts abound. Christianity in Nigeria—even in the shadow of Boko Haram and other jihadist militants[7]—has expanded to more than eighty million. This figure is half of the nation's population.[8] Florence Taylor points out that

> Muslims are converting to Christianity in northern Nigeria amid rapidly rising levels of Christian persecution, which has seen more than ten thousand Christians killed in five years.[9]

While there is brutal persecution, opponents cannot halt the expanding revival. The Pew Research Center points out that

> There are more Christians in Nigeria than in any single nation in traditionally Christian Western Europe. In fact, Nigeria's Christian population is

[6.] Kelly Head, "Living From His Presence," *The Voice* (March 13, 2014).

[7.] Florence Taylor, "Muslims Converting to Christianity in Nigeria, despite brutal persecution," *Christianity Today* (February 24, 2016).

[8.] "Global Christianity: Regional Distribution of Christians," Pew Research Center (December 19, 2011). http://www.pewforum.org/2011/12/19/global-christianity-regions.

[9.] Florence Taylor, "Muslims Converting to Christianity in Nigeria, Despite Brutal Persecution," *Christianity Today* (February 24, 2016).

nearly the same size as the total population of Germany.[10]

Much of this growth has taken place since the 1960s, originating in evangelical student revivals and later advancing through charismatic church plants.[11]

Multitudes have embraced dynamic worship forms. Rodney Stark points out that 90 percent of Nigeria attends Christian services weekly.[12] It's almost like the entire country is worshipping Jesus.

A similar spiritual fervor is evident in the nation of Kenya. Despite pushback from tribal leaders and al-Shabaab, an Islamic militant group, 85 percent of the population identifies with Christianity.[13]

The church, astonishingly, was not prominent in this nation until after it received independence from the United Kingdom in 1964. But since that time, several revivals have

---

[10.] Various, "Global Christianity: Regional Distribution of Christians," *Pew Research Center* (December 19, 2011). http://www.pewforum.org/2011/12/19/global-christianity-regions.

[11.] Various, "Spirit and Power – A 10-Country Survey of Pentecostals, - Historical Overview of Pentecostalism in Nigeria," *Pew Research Center* (October 5, 2006). http://www.pewforum.org/2006/10/05/historical-overview-of-pentecostalism-in-nigeria/.

[12.] Rodney Stark, *Triumph Of Faith: Why The World Is More Religious Than Ever* (Intercollegiate Studies Institute, 2015), 125.

[13.] Various, "Spirit and Power – A 10-Country Survey of Pentecostals," *Pew Research Center* (October 5, 2006). Retrieved from: http://www.pewforum.org/2006/10/05/spirit-and-power.

ensued.[14] Many Kenyans exhibit an intense hunger for the movement of the Holy Spirit.

Rodney Stark suggests that "nowhere has the global religious awakening been more dramatic than in Sub-Sahara Africa."[15] Over five hundred million people from this region have passionately embraced Jesus.[16] Wes Granberg-Michaelson of *The Washington Post* points out that these numbers will likely increase another 40 percent by 2030.[17]

Northern Africa

Northern Africa, a region traditionally antagonistic to Christianity, is also experiencing a resurgence of faith. In this tumultuous territory, many are coming to know the love of Jesus.

Bassam Michael Madany writes, "in recent years a phenomenon has occurred in North Africa that has even received public attention in the Arab press. It is the rebirth of

---

[14.] "Christianity in Kenya," *The Oxford Dictionary of the Christian Church, eds. F. L. Cross and E. A. Livingstone (New York:* Oxford University Press, 2005).

[15.] Rodney Stark, *Triumph Of Faith: Why The World Is More Religious Than Ever* (Intercollegiate Studies Institute, 2015), 107.

[16.] Various, "Spirit and Power – A 10-Country Survey of Pentecostals," *Pew Research Center* (October 5, 2006), http://www.pewforum.org/2006/10/05/spirit-and-power.

[17.] Wes Granberg-Michaelson, "Think Christianity is Dying? No, Christianity is Shifting Dramatically," *The Washington Post* (May 20, 2015).

Christianity."[18] Some are calling these men and women the "New Christians of North Africa."[19]

George Thomas points out,

> A Christian revival is touching the northernmost reaches of Africa. In a region once hostile to the gospel, now tens of thousands of Muslims are following Jesus. As the sun sets over the Mediterranean Sea, Muslims across Northern Africa are converting to faith in Jesus Christ in record numbers . . . . What experts say is that there is a profound move of God in the predominantly Muslim nations of Mauritania, Western Sahara, Morocco, Algeria, Libya, and Tunisia.[20]

There are increasing numbers of Christ-followers in the war-torn nation of Sudan. In the midst of "indiscriminate bombings, the burning, and looting of villages, killings, abductions, rapes, and arbitrary arrests,"[21] the church is expanding. Joel Rosenberg writes,

---

[18.] Bassam Michael Madany, "Muslims Converting To Christ: A Sign of the Times," Academia.edu (November 26, 2018).

[19.] Ibid.

[20.] George Thomas, "Revival Breaks Out In Land Once Hostile To Christianity," *CBN News*, April 22, 2014.

[21.] Various, "U.S. State Department Annual Report on Religious Freedom 2000," Bureau of Democracy, Human Rights, and Labor U.S. Department of State (September 5, 2000).

> One million Sudanese have turned to Christ since
> the year 2000—not in spite of persecution, war, and
> genocide, but because of them . . . . The estimated
> total number of believers in the country is more
> than 5.5 million.[22]

The brutalities that the Sudanese people have endured have
become a catalyst for expansion and growth. Rather than inhibiting
the work of the gospel, these hardships have propelled it.

The church is also on the rise in other parts of Northern
Africa. Since the beginning of the twenty-first century, thousands
of Algerians have been leaving Islam and placing their faith in
Christ.[23] This is a phenomenon that is grudgingly acknowledged by
the government.[24]

Although "no official census exists that would reveal the
actual number of people who have embraced Christianity," [25]
experts concede that "there is a noticeable rise" in the number of
Christians.[26]

Jalal Mousa, Salaf Rahmouni, and Naseema Raqiq,
suggested that Islam is, on average, losing at least "six individuals

---

[22.] Joel C. Rosenberg. *Inside the Revival: Good News and Changed Hearts Since 9/11* (Carol Stream, Illinois: Tyndale Publishers, 2009), 6.

[23.] See unnamed correspondent, "Christians Face Trial in Algeria over Wife's Accusations of Evangelizing," *Morning Star News* (October 10, 2018).

[24.] Elaph (November 13, 2012) quoted in Bassam Michael Madany, "Muslims Converting To Christ: A Sign of the Times," *Academia.edu* (November 26, 2018).

[25.] Ibid.

[26.] Ibid.

per day." The Muslim analysts are worried that thousands of Algerians are joining the church.[27]

It is evident that Christian congregations are gaining a foothold in Algeria. One pastor explained, "Every three months, the church holds baptisms, sometimes for more than 100 people."[28] The wonder of the gospel is transforming myriads of people.

Other nations have similar experiences. In Morocco, masses are converting to Christianity.[29] For the first the first time in centuries, Islam no longer has a stranglehold. Multitudes are wrestling with the claims of the Bible.

Many are convinced that Morocco is teetering on the edge of a spiritual awakening. Across the rugged terrain, the gospel is taking root, and multitudes are discovering the reality of God's kingdom.

Due to persecution from Islamic authorities in this region, new converts

> worship privately or at clandestine meetings in nondescript buildings, usually a private home. Small groups may come together in apartments to

---

[27.] Jalal Mousa, Salaf Rahmouni, and Naseema Raqiq quoted in Elaph (November 13, 2012) quoted in Bassam Michael Madany, "Muslims Converting To Christ: A Sign of the Times," *Academia.edu* (November 26, 2018).

[28.] Salah Kessai quoted in Mark, Ellis, "Algeria: Church Growing Rapidly Despite Obstacles," *God Reports* (October 8, 2018).

[29.] Sarah Williams, "Why Are There Hidden Christian Communities in Morocco?," *Culture Trip* (October 27, 2017).

pray, sing hymns, study the Bible, and discuss various religious and social matters.[30]

Tino Qahoush, an analyst and filmmaker, has been traveling across this territory to document the burgeoning revival. Describing some of his first-hand observations, he noted the following:

> What God is doing in North Africa, all the way from Mauritania to Libya is unprecedented in the history of missions. I have the privilege of recording testimonies and listening to firsthand stories of men and women, of all ages.[31]

The religious shift across this continent has been colossal, reordering the lives of millions of people. Multitudes are coming alive as they abandon Islam and animistic tribal religions. The goodness and grace of Jesus is transforming entire cultures. Africa is the future of global Christendom.

[30.] Unnamed correspondent, "Christians Face Trial in Algeria over Wife's Accusations of Evangelizing," *Morning Star News* (October 10, 2018).

[31.] Tino Qahoush quoted in George Thomas, "Revival Breaks Out In Land Once Hostile To Christianity," *CBN News* (April 22, 2014).

10. BURNING RING OF FIRE

CHRISTIANITY'S EXPANSION IN LATIN AMERICA

"The LORD has demonstrated his holy power before
the eyes of all the nations. All the ends of the earth
will see the victory of our God."

(ISAIAH 52:10 NLT)

Darkest Africa is not the only continent experiencing unprecedented advancement, but vast stretches of Latin America are encountering a similar impact. Millions of people are being awakened to the reality of the Holy Spirit. Lee Grady, former editor of *Charisma Magazine*, asserts, "There's a sovereign openness to the gospel in Latin America."[1]

Jon Mark Ruthven, a gifted professor from Regent University, and Randy Clark, a globally recognized missionary-evangelist, told me about the extraordinary move of God in Brazil. In city-wide crusades, tens of thousands are delivered from addictions and the works of darkness. Upstart congregations are expanding to ten thousand members in less than a year. What is happening there is extraordinary.

In 2013, I had the opportunity to travel to Argentina and witness firsthand what God is doing in this part of the globe. People lined up to get into church. There was spiritual hunger unlike anything I have ever witnessed. This whole region was ablaze with revival.

According to the Pew Research Center, evangelical Christians in Latin America have increased over 877 percent since 1900.[2] Astounding shifts are transpiring across the continent and millions of people are coming into the Kingdom of God.

In the midst of these changes, Traditional forms of Roman Catholicism are losing influence. Franz Damen, a Jesuit researcher, points out, "every hour on average 400 Catholics join Protestant

---

1. Lee Grady quoted in Jennifer LeClaire, "Sustained Revival Ignites Holy Ghost Transformation in Latin America" Charisma News (August 9, 2016).

2. Various, "Statistics," Pew Research Center, www.pewforum.org/Christian/Global-Christianity-exec.aspx.

sects."[3] The current growth rate of Evangelicalism[4] is three times that of Catholicism.[5]

Part of the reason for Protestant ascendancy, according to Campos Machado of the Federal University of Rio, is that evangelicals "go where the State does not meet the basic demands of the most needy."[6]

Many are persuaded that Evangelicalism has "revolutionary potential."[7] They believe that it is uniquely positioned "to bring hope, a new form of democracy, and solutions to many Latin American problems."[8]

However, it has been said that a rising tide lifts all boats. The revival is not only driving the growth of Protestantism but also renewing lackadaisical Catholicism. Traditional churches are also experiencing renewal. The Latin American world is embracing treasures old and new.

---

3. Roger Aubry, La misión: siguiendo a Jesús por los caminos de América Latina (Buenos Aires: Guadalupe, 1990), 105-115.

4. The term "Evangelical" refers to those who identify with mainline and evangelical Protestant denominations—as well as those who belong to Pentecostal denominations.

5. See Wes Granberg-Michaelson, "Think Christianity is Dying? No, Christianity is Shifting Dramatically," The Washington Post (May 20, 2015).

6. Professor Campos Machado, of the Religion, Gender, Social Action and Politics department of the School of Social Services of the Federal University of Rio quoted in Editor, "Peru, Brazil and Costa Rica exemplify the growing evangelical influence in Latin America," *Evangelical Focus* (March 1, 2018).

7. Milton Acosta, "Power Pentecostalisms: The 'non-Catholic' Latin American church is going full steam ahead—but are we on the right track?," *Christianity Today* (July 29, 2009).

8. Ibid.

Central America

The global South is teeming with life. The unprecedented expansion of renewalist Christianity is evidenced throughout Central America. A majority of the developing nations are at least 15 to 30 percent Protestant.[9]

For example, in Honduras, Nicaragua and El Salvador, over one-third of the population is caught up in this expanding move of God.[10] Across the barrios, families are encountering the fervency of revival. The sick and marginalized are coming face-to-face with the goodness and mercy of Jesus.

In Guatemala, a new church opens up every single day. Statistics confirm that 60 percent of the populace identifies with the emerging expressions of Christianity.[11] Thousands are being transformed through the passion and fervency of Spirit-filled worship.

Renewalist churches are often adding "support, and something more psychological."[12] These congregations allow

---

[9] Henri Gooren, "The Growth and Development of Non-Catholic Churches in Paraguay," *Spirit and Power: The Growth and Global Impact of Pentecostalism*, eds., Donald E, Miller, Kimon H. Sargeant, and Richard Flory (New York, Oxford University Press, 2013), 83.

[10] See Daniel Snyder, "The Growing Protestant Presence in Latin America," *Panoramas*, (January 11, 2017), http://www.panoramas.pitt.edu/art-and-culture/growing-protestant-presence-latin-america.

[11] John C. Green, "Pentecostal Growth and Impact in Latin America, Africa, and Asia" in *Spirit and Power: The Growth and Global Impact of Pentecostalism*, eds. Donald E. Miller, Kimon H. Sargeant, Richard Flory (New York: Oxford University Press, 2013), 331.

[12] Amy Bracken, "Did War Change Guatemala's Faith?," *PRI* (June 30, 2016).

people to have a badly needed catharsis. One Guatemalan missionary asserted that their worship services are "the only place where you can cry and yell."[13] Christianity is creating a context for self-actualization. Many are discovering a sense of identity through the death and resurrection of Jesus Christ. People throughout Central America are being awakened to all that God has for them.

South America

Peering further into South America, the impact is equally noteworthy. In Chile, evangelicalism is reordering the lives of multitudes.[14] A fiery revival erupted in the 1970s that spread through the nation and impacted other countries.[15] Tens of thousands are now encountering the saving power of Jesus.[16]

A similar outworking is evidenced in other nations. For example, Columbia and Argentina are seeing thousands renounce violence, drugs, and ancestral superstitions as the work of the Spirit expands. Myriads of new congregations are being established.

---

[13] Steve Elliot quoted in Amy Bracken, "Did War Change Guatemala's Faith?," *PRI* (June 30, 2016).

[14.] See Roger Aubry, *La misión: siguiendo a Jesús por los caminos de América Latina* (Buenos Aires: Guadalupe, 1990), 106. Also see

http://evangelicalfocus.com/blogs/3010/The_exodus_of_nominal_Catholics_to_the_ranks_of_Protestant_churches_in_Latin_America#_edn6.

[15.] Philip Jenkins, "Why Chile has Pentecostal Bishops," *The Christian Century* (June 2, 2017).

[16.] Various, "Spirit and Power: A 10 Country Survey of Pentecostals - Overview: Pentecostalism in Latin America," *Pew Research Center* (October 5, 2006), http://www.pewforum.org/2006/10/05/overview-pentecostalism-in-latin-america/

Rebounding from turmoil and economic duress, Peru is coming alive. A thundering chorus of millions is singing about the magnificence of Jesus. Richard Daigle notes,

> Peru has been a spiritual revival that has seen the estimated number of born-again Christians rise dramatically. . . . Peru's evangelical population grew from single digits to 12.5 percent in 2007. The official 2013 estimate is 17 percent, but the actual number may well be over 20 percent.[17]

What is transpiring in Brazil is even more gripping. Before 1970, less than 3 percent of the population was evangelical. Now over half embrace this religious identity. For Protestantism to go from 2 percent to 50 percent in a rigidly Roman Catholic nation in less than fifty years is extraordinary. Paul Strand observes that

> Christianity is increasing in Brazil. If the trend continues, it is predicted that more than half of all Brazilians (109 million Christians out of 209 million citizens) will be evangelical Christians by 2020 . . . . Brazil is a land in revival.[18]

[17.] Richard Daigle, "After Many Prophecies, Peru Sees Spiritual, Economic Revival," *Charisma News* (January 24, 2013).

[18.] Paul Strand, "Spirit-Led Revival Movement Sweeps Brazil," *CBN News* (March 11, 2011).

Fervent forms of Christianity are transforming communities across stretches of South America. Millions of people are being brought into the kingdom. [19]

Shifting Center of Gravity

The center of gravity has already moved. Wes Granberg-Michaelson, of *The Washington Post*, pointed out that, "in 1980, more Christians were found in the global South than the North for the first time in 1,000 years."[20] Samuel Rodriguez, president of the National Hispanic Christian Leadership Conference, said, "The majority of Christ-followers around the world are now Latinos."[21]

Analysts from the Pew Research Center point out that this growth "cannot be explained fully by demographic factors, such as fertility rates or immigration."[22] The most logical source for these changes is spiritual awakening. Lee Grady writes,

"There is a move of God sweeping so many parts of Latin America . . . . I have yet to go to any place in

---

[19] Various, "Spirit and Power: A 10 Country Survey of Pentecostals - Overview: Pentecostalism in Latin America," *Pew Research Center* (October 5, 2006). http://www.pewforum.org/2006/10/05/overview-pentecostalism-in-latin-america/

[20] Wes Granberg-Michaelson, "Think Christianity is dying? No, Christianity is shifting dramatically," *The Washington Post* (May 20, 2015).

[21] Samuel Rodriguez quoted in Jennifer LeClaire, "Sustained Revival Ignites Holy Ghost Transformation in Latin America" *Charisma News* (August 9, 2016).

[22] Various, "Brazil's Changing Religious Landscape," Pew Research Center (July 18, 2013), http://www.pewforum.org/2013/07/18/brazils-changing-religious-landscape.

a major metropolitan area where there's not an outpouring of the Holy Spirit." [23]

Jennifer LeClaire was astonished by what she encountered in the emerging Latin world. While witnessing massive worship gatherings, she noted the following:

> The Holy Spirit is raining down on Latin America with tens of thousands of people either laying prostrate on the ground or standing with hands raised as tears stream down their faces. [24]

An explosive spiritual awakening is underway. More than 156 million Latinos now practice renewalist forms of Christianity.[25] Some project that the figures are even higher.

The message of Jesus is reinvigorating third-world nations and transforming the global landscape. Latin America is already at the helm of Christianity's future.

[23.] Lee Grady quoted in Jennifer LeClaire, "Sustained Revival Ignites Holy Ghost Transformation in Latin America," *Charisma News* (August 9, 2016).

[24.] Jennifer LeClaire, "Sustained Revival Ignites Holy Ghost Transformation in Latin America," *Charisma News* (August 9, 2016).

[25.] Ibid.

11. AN EAST WIND BLOWING:

CHRISTIANITY'S EXPANSION IN ASIA

*"I will gather all nations and peoples together, and
they will see my glory."*

(ISAIAH 66:18B NLT)

An underground Chinese pastor came to the United States for a season and enrolled in the Revival Training Center. After some classes, we discussed what was transpiring in Asia.

Although the government continues to crack down on churches, he told me that officials could not stay on top of the explosive church growth. Thousands of upstart congregations were popping up all over China.

He said, "No one can stop what God is doing. Jesus is bringing his light to millions of hungry people. In the future, many new missionaries will come from China."

Christianity's progression in this faraway place is astounding. Throughout the Asian landmass, millions are forging a new pathway. Many are encountering the beauty and wonder of the kingdom of God.

Unprecedented Stirrings

Spiritual hunger is stirring. In the Philippines, on the edge of Asia, 85 percent of the population identifies with Jesus. This emerging nation is "home to more than 4 percent of the world's Christians, perhaps 85 million strong."[1] The Philippines will likely have substantial influence in this region in decades ahead.

The church is advancing in other places as well. In 1920, only three hundred thousand believers lived in all of Korea. After being split in two in the 1950s, Christianity continued to expand. Presently more than fifteen million believers reside in South Korea[2] and nine million in North Korea, arguably the "most oppressive place in the world."[3] The flames of revival are raging on both sides of the border.

---

[1] Philip Jenkins, "The Future of Christianity in Asia," *Aletia* (August 21, 2014), https://aleteia.org/2014/08/21/the-future-of-christianity-in-asia/.

[2] Ibid.

[3] Hollie McKay, "North Korea: How Christians Survive in the World's Most Anti-Christian Nation," *Fox News* (August 18, 2017).

Unprecedented stirrings are underway in other parts of this region. From 1965-1985, about 2.5 million Indonesian Muslims converted to Christianity.[4] Although possessing a sizeable Islamic population, this nation currently has more than 30 million believers.[5]

The impact is being witnessed in other countries as well. Although known as the "missionaries' graveyard," Christianity is experiencing growth among young adults in Japan.[6] Congregations are struggling here, but spiritual stirrings are beginning to draw attention.[7]

Although the 1.3 billion people who live in India are predominately Hindu, more than 60 million Christians call this nation home.[8] The growth of the church has not pleased everyone. Bands of Hindu militants have reacted violently, burning homes and decimating sanctuaries. Out of the fifty countries where

---

[4] David B. Barrett, George Thomas Kurian, and Todd M. Johnson, eds. *World Christian Encyclopedia* (Oxford University Press, 2001), 374.

[5] Philip Jenkins, "The Future of Christianity in Asia," *Aletia* (August 21, 2014), https://aleteia.org/2014/08/21/the-future-of-christianity-in-asia/. Also see Various, "Global Christianity: Regional Distribution of Christians," Pew Research Center (December 19, 2011). http://www.pewforum.org/2011/12/19/global-christianity-regions.

[6] Editor, "Christianity on Upswing in Japan: Gallup Poll: Traditional Religions Show Decline Among Teens," *World News Daily* (March 18, 2018), http://www.wnd.com/2006/03/35319/.

[7] See Rodney Stark, *Triumph Of Faith: Why The World Is More Religious Than Ever* (Intercollegiate Studies Institute, 2015), 157.

[8] David B. Barrett, George Thomas Kurian, and Todd M. Johnson, eds. *World Christian Encyclopedia* (Oxford University Press, 2001), 374.

persecution is at its worst, India comes in at number eleven.[9] Although harassment rages, God is still at work.

Pastor Joseph D'Souza declared, "Persecution has never stopped the growth of the church. In fact, when we are attacked, when we are persecuted, we become stronger."[10]

In Singapore, Christians now make up at least 20 percent of the population.[11] Some of the churches have "grown so large they are meeting at stadiums and convention centers."[12]

Currently, 10 percent of Hong Kong and 9 percent of Malaysia identifies with Christianity.[13] In addition, over eight million followers of Jesus reside in Vietnam.[14] We see a myriad of examples of the triumph of the church in this region. Asia is coming alive with the gospel.

[9.] See Emily Jones, "Persecution is Rising in India, but Christianity Standing Strong," *CBN News* (January 16, 2018), http://www1.cbn.com/cbnnews/cwn/2018/january/persecution-is-rising-in-india-but-christianity-standing-strong.

[10.] Joseph D'Souza quoted in Emily Jones, "Persecution is Rising in India, but Christianity Standing Strong," *CBN News* (January 16, 2018).

[11.] See Kenny Chee, "Better Educated Singapore Residents Look to Religion," *Asia One News* (January 13, 2011).

[12.] Donald E. Miller, "Introduction: Pentecostalism As a Global Phenomenon," *Spirit and Power: The Growth and Global Impact of Pentecostalism*, eds., Donald E, Miller, Kimon H. Sargeant, and Richard Flory (New York, Oxford University Press, 2013), 10.

[13.] See William Kay," Gifts of the Spirit: Reflections on Pentecostalism and Its Growth in Asia," *Spirit and Power: The Growth and Global Impact of Pentecostalism*, eds., Donald E, Miller, Kimon H. Sargeant, and Richard Flory (New York, Oxford University Press, 2013), 268.

[14.] Philip Jenkins, "The Future of Christianity in Asia," *Aletia* (August 21, 2014). https://aleteia.org/2014/08/21/the-future-of-christianity-in-asia/.

China's Spiritual Awakening

Although faith is taking root across the continent, it is spreading the fastest in the People's Republic of China. This nation only had one million Christians in 1949. Now there are more than fifty-eight million.[15]

Fenggang Yang, an expert on religion in China, is convinced that the number of believers will swell even more in the coming years. He observes,

> By 2030, China's total Christian population would exceed 247 million, placing it above Mexico, Brazil, and the United States as the largest Christian congregation in the world.[16]

Other researchers are also acknowledging the rapid expansion of Christianity. One reputable English newspaper published the following:

> Estimates of the number of Christians in China today vary between 60 million and 120 million, which would suggest as many as one in ten of the population are already believers. It has been predicted that by 2030 there could be almost a

---

[15.] Tom Phillips, "China On Course To Become 'World's Most Christian Nation' Within 15 years," *London Telegraph* (April 19, 2014).

[16.] Fenggang Yang quoted in Tom Phillips, "China On Course To Become 'World's Most Christian Nation' within 15 years," *London Telegraph* (April 19, 2014).

quarter of a billion Christians in China making it the biggest Christian population in the world.[17]

Most analysts are too conservative. If house church participants and those across rural China are included, as much as 20 percent of the nation already identifies with Jesus. This would be astounding because, before 1970, there were no legally functioning churches in China.[18]

Admittedly, it's difficult to determine the actual figures. Most believers are reluctant to publicly acknowledge their faith because they fear "government reprisal."[19] Though greater freedoms are emerging, the followers of Jesus still experience persecution.

Although it's impossible to put our finger on the numbers, it's clear that "more Christian believers are found worshipping in China on any given Sunday than in the United States."[20]

The church has made significant inroads in this once closed-off nation. This Asian giant has been awakened. Rodney Stark reiterates that the People's Republic of China will be "playing a significant role in the global religious awakening."[21]

[17.] John Bingham, "Justin Welby Ponders Landmark China Tour to see the Explosion of Christianity," *The Telegraph*, December 14, 2014.

[18.] Mark Noll, "Faith and Conflict: The Global Rise of Christianity," Council on Foreign Relations and Pew Research Center (March 2, 2005).

[19.] Bill Murphy, "China, Officially Atheist, Could have more Christians than the U.S. by 2030," *Houston Chronicle* (February 24, 2018).

[20.] Wes Granberg-Michaelson, "Think Christianity is Dying? No, Christianity is Shifting Dramatically," *The Washington Post* (May 20, 2015).

[21.] Rodney Stark, *Triumph Of Faith: Why The World Is More Religious Than Ever* (Intercollegiate Studies Institute, 2015), 158.

Center of Global Christianity?

Across the vast expanse of Asia, faith is surging. Signs of awakening are everywhere. Hundreds of millions have come into the kingdom. William Kay writes,

> Because of their geographical location, demographic trajectory, and economic strength, churches in these areas can be seen as crucial to the shape of world Christianity as the 21st century progresses.[22]

Many expect the Asian Church to expand even more in the next few decades. In the last century, Christianity grew at twice the rate of population. The church is gaining inestimable influence in this burgeoning region.

The global East currently holds an eighth of the worldwide Christian community.[23] Within a decade, it will be considerably higher. Wes Granberg-Michaelson points out that "Asia's Christian population of 350 million is projected to grow to 460 million by 2025."[24]

Journalist Masako Fukui declared, "No doubt about it, Christianity is big in Asia." So many are following Jesus that this

---

[22.] William Kay, "Gifts of the Spirit: Reflections on Pentecostalism and Its Growth in Asia," *Spirit and Power: The Growth and Global Impact of Pentecostalism*, eds., Donald E, Miller, Kimon H. Sargeant, and Richard Flory (New York, Oxford University Press, 2013), 268.

23. See Philip Jenkins, "The Future of Christianity in Asia," Aletia (August 21, 2014), https://aleteia.org/2014/08/21/the-future-of-christianity-in-asia/.

24. Ibid.

century might ultimately be described as "the Asian Christian Century."[25]

In 1910, there were only twenty-seven million Christians across the world's largest land mass.[26] Now there are close to half a billion. A land that was once opposed to the gospel will likely be the center of it in our lifetime.

[25] Masako Fukui, "The Rise of Christianity in Asia, ABC News Australia," (December 2, 2014), http://www.abc.net.au/radionational/programs/archived/encounter/the-rise-of-christianity-in-asia/5934564.

[26] Various, "Global Christianity—A Report on the Size and Distribution of the World's Christian Population," *Pew Research Center* (December 19, 2011).

12. THE DESERT IS AN OCEAN:

CHRISTIANITY'S EXPANSION IN THE MIDDLE EAST

"May God be gracious to us and bless us, and cause
His face to shine upon us, Selah that your ways may
be known on earth, your salvation among all
nations."

(PSALM 67:1-2 NIV)

A young Iranian father visited our church last year with his wife and daughter. He was in the United States studying for the ministry. I enjoyed his enthusiasm as he talked about the work of Jesus in his nation.

He acknowledged that an underground revival taking place in the Middle East is bringing tens of thousands into the kingdom.

In spite of severe persecution and violence, Christianity is beginning to make incredible strides.

Thousands of Muslims have come into the church over recent decades.[1] Missiologists have pointed out that more from an Islamic background "have committed to follow Christ in the last 10 years than in the last 15 centuries."[2] In spite of persecution, assassinations, and church bombings, a glorious revival is expanding in the Islamic territories.

One report estimates that ten million individuals from Muslim backgrounds currently identify with Christianity.[3] Other analysts suggest that as many as twenty million believers now live in the war-torn Middle East. The particulars can be debated, but in the Mediterranean world, Christianity is making extraordinary inroads.

A Middle Eastern Revival

Joel Rosenberg has documented the growth of Christianity in the Middle East. Through first-hand reconnaissance and reports

[1] See reports in David Garrison, *A Wind In The House Of Islam: How God Is Drawing Muslims Around The World To Faith In Jesus Christ* (WIGTake Resources, 2014).

[2] Audrey Lee, "Why Revival is Exploding Among Muslims," *Charisma* (December 2012).

[3] See Duane Alexander Miller and Patrick Johnstone, "Believers in Christ from a Muslim Background: A Global Census," *Interdisciplinary Journal of Research on Religion* 11 (2015): 10. Also Timothy C. Morgan, "Why Muslims are Becoming the Best Evangelists: Missiologist Dave Garrison Documents Global Surge in Muslims Leading Muslims to Christ. He calls it, 'Unprecedented,'" *Christianity Today* (April 22, 2014).

from indigenous leaders, he is convinced that Christianity is increasing.

Pakistan is not typically associated with Christian revival. Nevertheless, something is beginning to spark in this ancient land. Despite the violence against the minority Christian populace, churches are expanding. Rosenberg recounts the following:

> Senior Pakistani Christian leaders tell me there is a "conversion explosion" going on in their country. There are now an estimated 2.5 million to 3 million born-again Pakistani believers worshiping Jesus Christ. Whole towns and villages along the Afghan-Pakistani border are . . . converting to Christianity.[4]

What is occurring in Pakistan isn't unusual. Other Arabic countries are experiencing similar outpourings.

In Iran, Christianity is also surging. Despite brutal persecution, the Evangelical population is one of the fastest growing in the world.[5] Over the last twenty years, multitudes have turned to Jesus.

Before the Islamic Revolution in 1979, there weren't many believers in that nation with a Muslim background. At that time,

---

[4] Joel C. Rosenberg, *Inside the Revival: Good News and Changed Hearts Since 9/11* (Wheaton: Tyndale Publishers, 2009), 15-16.

[5] Christian growth in Iran is currently estimated at 19.6% by Operation World. http://www.operationworld.org/.

there were less than five hundred known converts.[6] Today, over one million Iranians claim allegiance to Jesus.[7]

Christians in this nation must overcome innumerable obstacles. Many evade the reach of the Islamic militants by establishing a network of underground churches. Sadly, their efforts are not always successful.

Michael Nazir-Ali, speaking to the Council on Foreign Relations in Washington D.C., noted that Iranian believers "have been imprisoned, some have been killed – a very close friend of mine was killed. And they continue to thrive, even in a very unpromising situation."[8]

Shahrokh Afshar, an Iranian filmmaker, says that the government officials "know they can't stop Christianity from growing. They know the more pressure they put on people, the more people turn to Christ."[9]

In Saudi Arabia—the epicenter of Islam—the gospel is also taking root. Even with murderous threats, "the number of Saudi Muslims becoming Christians is increasing."[10]

[6.] Joel C. Rosenberg, *Inside the Revival: Good News and Changed Hearts Since 9/11* (Wheaton: Tyndale Publishers, 2009), 3.

[7.] Michael Ashcraft, "Christianity Exploding in Iran Despite Efforts of Government to Stamp it out," *God Reports* (August 4, 2017).

[8.] Michael Nazir-Ali, "Faith and Conflict: The Global Rise of Christianity," Council on Foreign Relations and Pew Research Center (March 2, 2005).

[9.] Shahrokh Afshar quoted in Michael Ashcraft, "Christianity Exploding in Iran Despite Efforts of Government to Stamp it out," *God Reports* (August 4, 2017).

[10.] Various, "'No Better Time' for Growth of Christianity in Saudi Arabia," *World Watch Monitor* (April 12, 2018).

The converts from Muslim backgrounds are forced to keep their loyalties hidden, holding worship services in homes and out-of-the-way places. In spite of the toxic culture, the church continues to grow. Rosenberg points out that

> Arab Christian leaders estimated there were more than one hundred thousand Saudi Muslim background believers in 2005, and they believe the numbers are even higher today.[11]

This oil-rich nation is encountering an unprecedented outpouring of the Holy Spirit. Pastor Emad Al Abdy reiterated that "there is no better time than now" for the growth of Christianity in Saudi Arabia.[12]

Other nations in the Middle East are also being awakened. Jayson Casper, a journalist with *Christianity Today*, highlighted some of the magnificent things taking place. He writes,

> Today the Pew Research Center numbers Christians in the Arabian Peninsula at 2.3 million - more Christians than nearly 100 countries can claim. The Gulf Christian Fellowship, an umbrella group, estimates 3.5 million . . . . United Arab Emirates Christian population . . . [is] 13 percent,

---

[11.] Joel C. Rosenberg, *Inside the Revival: Good News and Changed Hearts Since 9/11* (Wheaton: Tyndale Publishers, 2009), 13-14.

[12.] Various, "'No Better Time' for Growth of Christianity in Saudi Arabia," *World Watch Monitor* (April 12, 2018).

according to Pew. Among other Gulf states, Bahrain, Kuwait, and Qatar each about 14 percent Christian, while Oman is about 6 percent. Even Saudi Arabia, home to Islam's holiest cities (Mecca and Medina), is 4 percent Christian.[13]

An underground revival is underway in one of the most challenging regions on earth. In the face of severe bloodshed and persecution, thousands are turning to Jesus.[14] Believers across the Arabian Peninsula are convinced that millions of their countrymen will accept Christ.[15]

Darkness is Fading

God's grace is upending the Mediterranean world. This is a truth that Muslim clerics are even starting to recognize. In December 2001, Sheikh Ahmad al Qataani, president of the Companions Lighthouse for the Science of Islamic Law, appeared on a live interview on Al-Jazeera television. He declared the following:

> There are now 1.5 million churches whose congregations account for 46 million people. In

---

[13.] Jayson Casper, "Why Christianity Is Surging In The Heart Of Islam," *Christianity Today* 59:7 (September 2015): 19.

[14.] See Stoyan Zaimov, "Thousands of Muslims Reportedly Turning to Christ in Middle East," *Fox News* (January 11, 2017).

[15.] Ibid.

every hour, 667 Muslims convert to Christianity. Every day, 16,000 Muslims convert to Christianity. Every year, 6 million Muslims convert to Christianity. These numbers are very large indeed.[16]

Stunned, the interviewer interrupted the cleric. "Hold on! Let me clarify. Do we have six million converting from Islam to Christianity?" Al Qataani repeated his assertion. "Every year," the cleric confirmed, adding, "a tragedy has happened."[17]

Although Westerners remain apprehensive, Muslims are coming to Jesus by the thousands. Light expels the murky shadows, illuminating the darkest corners of the earth.

While Christian advancement in the Middle East is modest in comparison to what is happening in other parts of the globe, the children of Ishmael are experiencing unprecedented joy. Abraham's extended family is finding its way home.

[16.] Editor, "Al-Jazeerah: 6 Million Muslims Convert to Christianity in Africa each year," *Muslim Statistics* (December 14, 2012).
https://muslimstatistics.wordpress.com/2012/12/14/al-jazeerah-6-million-muslims-convert-to-christianity-in-africa-each-year. Al-Jazeera has since removed the interview and details.

[17.] Ibid.

It's time to acknowledge the inexplicable wonder of the kingdom of God. The dynamic expansion of Christianity is "one of the most important global developments in the modern world."[18]

[18.] Richard Flory and Kimon H. Sargeant, "Conclusion: Pentecostalism in Global Perspective," *Spirit and Power: The Growth and Global Impact of Pentecostalism*, eds., Donald E, Miller, Kimon H. Sargeant, and Richard Flory (New York, Oxford University Press, 2013), 298.

13. ALL IS QUIET ON THE WESTERN FRONT
CHRISTIANITY'S EXPANSION IN NORTH AMERICA AND EUROPE

"Some of you will rebuild the ancient ruins; you will restore the foundations laid long ago; you will be called the repairer of broken walls, the restorer of streets where people live."

(ISAIAH 58:12 NLT)

Traveling to a ministry engagement in California, I sat next to a university student on a connecting flight. I was reading Philip Jenkins notable work, *The Next Christendom: The Coming of Global Christianity.*

My seatmate asked me about the book. I was happy to discuss some of the ideas. Jenkins pointed out that while

Christianity's influence is diminishing in the United States and Europe, it is expanding in the developing world. He believes that the center of Christianity will shift in coming decades.

As we talked, the student mentioned his trip to Europe the previous summer. He said, "I witnessed, firsthand, Christianity's hollow shell. There were empty pews in opulent cathedrals. I'm not sure many Europeans still embrace the tenets of Christianity."

He acknowledged some of his own struggles. He said that he had grown up in a Christian home and had been active in youth programs. His spiritual fervency was high when he first entered college, but he did not remain passion-filled.

He made it clear that he still believed in Jesus but had numerous questions. He mentioned that he no longer trusted the church as an institution. This twenty-year-old was becoming what sociologist Grace Davie called a "believing non-belonger."[1] In many ways, he's a reflection of millions of others.

Although Christianity is overtaking the world, in North America and Europe, it's encountering an uphill battle. With tendencies toward skepticism and doubt, many Westerners no longer have a pervading sense of awe. Max Weber lamented, "The fate of our times is characterized by rationalization and intellectualization, and, above all, by the disenchantment of the world."[2]

---

[1] Grace Davie, *Religion in Britain since 1945* (Oxford: Blackwell, 1994).

[2] Max Weber, *Max Weber: Essays in Sociology*, translated and edited by H. H. Gerth and C. Wright Mills (New York: Oxford University Press, 1946), 155.

What's Going on?

I sat down for lunch with a group of Kansas City leaders to talk about Christianity's future. With millions being saved in the developing world, I thought that surely the West was experiencing some measure of impact.

I told my colleagues that Christian conversions are outpacing population growth across the globe. Nevertheless, North America and Europe aren't witnessing the same level of expansion. The Western church isn't shrinking, but it's not keeping up with escalating birth rates or changing demographics.

As I talked with my colleagues, I explained that we needed to regain a sense of hope. While the gospel isn't advancing as quickly in our part of the world, promising signs are emerging. Even in shadow, light illuminates. The glory of God is ever increasing.

Europe

I have friends who serve churches in Finland, the Netherlands, and the United Kingdom. They have recounted heartbreaking experiences. Many of their neighbors are ambivalent about the church.

Faith seems the bleakest where it was once the brightest. Centuries ago, Europe was the epicenter of Christianity.[3] Yet in

---

[3.] See Philip Jenkins, "In Europe, Even Occasional Prayer is on the Way Out," *Christian Century* (May 31, 2018)

the intervening years, skepticism and unrest have "produced empty church pews across the continent."[4]

In the confines of darkness, light shines the brightest. Although older liturgical forms are fading and traditional congregations aren't capturing the masses, all is not lost. Christianity has not been forsaken.

Most cannot see the contributions of the burgeoning renewalists,[5] independent congregations,[6] and innovative missionary enterprises.[7] Europe has been under siege, but the fire is increasing.

Renewalist congregations like Hope City London, Kensington Temple, and Hillsong Church London "are drawing people of all ages and races."[8] Their innovative worship services are influencing tens of thousands of people.

European cities are also receiving "reverse missionaries." Evangelists from Latin America, Africa, and Asia believe they're called to revitalize Western Christianity.[9] Their upstart

---

[4.] Colin Hansen, "European Christianity's 'Failure to Thrive,'" *Christianity Today* (August 2008).

[5.] See Dale Coulter, "A Charismatic Invasion of Anglicanism?" *First Things* (January 7, 2014).

[6.] See Aaqil Ahmed, "Christianity Isn't Dead—It Has Just Become More Diverse," *Independent* (Saturday, March 19, 2016).

[7.] See Matthew Bell, "Inside the Alpha Course - British Christianity's Biggest Success Story," *Independent* (Sunday, March 31, 2013).

[8.] Hazel Torres, "Christianity in U.K. Sees 'Seismic Shift' as Pentecostal and Charismatic Churches Thrive, Replacing Aging Churches," *Christian Today* (March 31, 2016).

[9.] See Lily Kuo, "Africa's 'Reverse Missionaries' are Bringing Christianity back to the United Kingdom," *Quartz* (October 11, 2017).

congregations are bustling with foreigners and native Europeans. The whole region is seeing advancements.

In Belgium, for example, Christianity has doubled since 1980. This is due, in part, to the African diaspora and the rise of independent congregations.[10]

The Ghanaian and Congolese churches are influencing thousands in Belgium. Traditional churches are also witnessing hints of resurgence. There is a new "dynamism that seems destined to leave its mark on post-Catholic secular Belgium."[11] Other parts of Europe are observing similar scenarios.

Negative reports don't always provide the whole picture. Few would claim that these men and women were devout, but 71 percent of Europe still self-identifies as Christian.[12]

More are enamored with doctrine than attending worship services.[13] Sidestepping spiritual matters, they tend to identify Christianity with textual studies. With an emphasis on theology, some have forgotten the magnificence of Jesus.

But hidden in the masses are catalysts who will take this continent into a new season of revival. The Lord has more in store for this land. Over recent decades, European Christianity has been

---

[10.] Colin Godwin, "The Recent Growth of Pentecostalism in Belgium," *International Bulletin of Missionary Research* 37:2 (April 2013): 90.

[11.] Ibid, 94.

[12.] Tom Heneghan, "Europe: Not as Secular as you Think," *Religious News Service* (May 29, 2018).

[13.] Rodney Stark, *Triumph Of Faith: Why The World Is More Religious Than Ever* (Intercollegiate Studies Institute, 2015), 44.

sluggish, but signs abound that a new era is unfolding. Aaqil Ahmed writes,

> Christianity is not in terminal decline as many would have us believe. It's just different now, and it's growing . . . . It may have been pronounced to be at death's door in the last century, but now it's firmly back in the public space.[14]

In the midst of tempest and toil, the wonder of the gospel continues to touch every corner of the world.

United States

Across the Atlantic, the United States has also entered the crucible. I have witnessed the struggle in dozens of congregations. Reports are suggesting that the American church is losing its hold on society. Sarah Pulliam Bailey of *The Washington Post* reiterates,

> Christianity is on the decline in America, not just among younger generations or in certain regions of the country but across race, gender, education, and geographic barriers. The percentage of adults who describe themselves as Christians dropped by nearly

---

[14.] Aaqil Ahmed, "Christianity isn't Dead—It has just Become More Diverse," *Independent* (Saturday, March 19, 2016).

eight percentage points in just seven years to about 71 percent.[15]

When discussing this with some colleagues, a few concerns came into focus. Local congregations are often distracted and caught up in the wrong kind of pursuits. Most are not paying attention, and have become entangled in marginal matters.

Moralism, nationalism, and family values hold prominence in our culture, but it's presumptuous to suggest that they're the essence of the New Testament. Although many are settling for less than their inheritance, God has not forgotten America.

The church is as impactful as ever but not as the religion people are accustomed to. In the twenty-first century, American Christianity is growing "in unexpected and surprising ways."[16]

Outside of the purview of the masses, the United States is "quickly changing faces." In the midst of plateauing "white, Western, majority culture Christianity,"[17] immigration is bringing thousands of believers here from the developing world. According to missiologist Keenan Cook, "The gospel may be spreading faster in your city in Spanish or Chinese right now than in English."[18]

[15] Sarah Pulliam Bailey, "Christianity Faces Sharp Decline as Americans are Becoming even less Affiliated with Religion," *Washington Post* (May 12, 2015).

[16] Keenan Cook, "The De-Europeanization of American Christianity," *The Send Institute* (April 3, 2018).

[17] Ibid.

[18] Ibid.

Throughout the West, Christianity is undergoing an ethnic transformation. This unforeseen development is already impacting many of the older denominations. Darren Rogers writes,

> Much of the numerical growth in the Assemblies of God in recent decades has been among ethnic minorities. From 2001 to 2015, the number of AG adherents increased by 21.5%. During this period, the number of white adherents decreased by 1.6% and the number of non-white adherents increased by 76.8%.[19]

Immigrants and minorities will continue to shape the future of Christianity. Millions of people outside of the Western European ethos are coming to know Jesus.

Faith is expanding in other remarkable ways. Independent and renewalist congregations are being activated. Pastors, prayer leaders, and influencers are uniting together as a network of independent leaders, focusing "on spreading beliefs and practices through media, conferences, and ministry schools."[20]

For example, Bethel Church in Redding, California, the International House of Prayer in Kansas City, Missouri, HRock

---

[19.] Darren Rogers, "Assemblies of God 2015 Statistics Released, Growth Spurred by Ethnic Transformation," *Flower Pentecostal Heritage Center* (June 24, 2016).

[20.] Brad Christerson and Richard Flory, "How a Christian Movement is Growing Rapidly in the Midst of Religious Decline," *Salon* (March 21, 2017).

Church in Pasadena, California, and other high-profile ministries are drawing millions to the faith.[21]

In addition to an expansive online reach, renewalist leaders are organizing large-scale gatherings. Azusa Now at the Los Angeles Coliseum and Awaken the Dawn at the National Mall in Washington D.C., brought together over fifty thousand people in 2017.[22] Multitudes are embracing Christianity through these efforts.

Congregations within the renewalist persuasion are the fastest growing segment of Christianity in America. As attendance at traditional Protestant churches shrank .05 percent a year from 1970 to 2010, renewalist congregations saw an average increase of 3.24 percent.[23]

People insist that the United States has rejected the faith of their fathers, but this judgment is wrong. A vast majority believes in God with less than 4 percent professing atheism.[24] Few would claim an exemplary life, but 80 percent persist in their Christian identification.[25]

[21.] Bob Smietana, "The 'Prophets' and 'Apostles' Leading the Quiet Revolution in American Religion," *Christianity Today* (August 3, 2017).

[22.] Ibid.

[23.] Brad Christerson and Richard Flory, "How a Christian Movement is Growing Rapidly in the Midst of Religious Decline," *Salon* (March 21, 2017).

[24.] This is a figure that hasn't increased since 1944. Rodney Stark, *Triumph Of Faith: Why The World Is More Religious Than Ever* (Intercollegiate Studies Institute, 2015), 190.

[25.] Ibid., 185.

At least half pray daily,[26] and a high percentage acknowledged to the Gallup organization that they were "very conscious of the presence of God."[27]

Also, sanctuaries aren't as empty as some believe. Attendance numbers "though over reported are not changing substantially."[28] Those who attend services more than once a week continue to hold steady.[29]

When considering the penetration of Christianity in America, it's important to point out that tens of thousands are absent from any church rolls. For this segment, going to a conference a few times a year provides the necessary "jolt." This is, for them, "the new rhythm, as opposed the weekly rhythm of church life."[30]

A research team from Harvard and Indiana University affirm, "The intensity of American religion is persistent and exceptional." It is not becoming "irrelevant or any less intense."[31]

---

[26] Ibid.

[27] Baylor University, *The Baylor Religion Survey, Wave II* (Waco, Texas: Baylor Institute for Studies of Religion, 2007). The Gallup Organization conducted this survey.

[28] Ed Stetzer, "Nominals to Nones: 3 Key Takeaways from Pew's Religious Landscape Survey," *Christianity Today* (May 12, 2015).

[29] Landon Schnabel and Sean Bock, "The Persistent and Exceptional Intensity of American Religion: A Response to Recent Research," *Sociological Science* 4 (November 2017): 697.

[30] Bob Smietana, "The 'Prophets' and 'Apostles' Leading the Quiet Revolution in American Religion," *Christianity Today* (August 3, 2017).

[31] Landon Schnabel and Sean Bock, "The Persistent and Exceptional Intensity of American Religion: A Response to Recent Research," *Sociological Science* 4 (November 2017): 697.

Along similar lines, prominent evangelical analyst Ed Stetzer noted the following:

> We are not seeing the death of Christianity in America, but we are seeing remarkable changes. Culture is shifting and the religious landscape is evolving. But, instead of the funeral of a religion, at least in part we are witnessing the demise of casual and cultural Christianity. And that is not necessarily a bad thing.[32]

While those who possess faith are increasing in devotion, nominal churchgoers are racing for the back door. Rather than being rejected, Christianity is being refined. Many inexplicable wonders lie ahead.

The celebrated novelist, Charles Dickens, once wrote, "There are dark shadows on the earth, but its lights are stronger in the contrast."[33] We cannot lose sight of what is happening. Within crumbling ashes, God is rekindling a dying ember. North America and Europe are beginning to experience a startling resurgence. The West is on the verge of a mighty awakening.

---

[32] Ed Stetzer, "The State of The Church in America: When Numbers Point To A New Reality, Part 2," *Christianity Today* (September 14, 2016).

[33] Charles Dickens, *The Pickwick Papers* (London: Chapman and Hall, 1837), 518.

14. EVEN DARKNESS MUST PASS
CONCLUDING A MARVELOUS JOURNEY

"The whole earth is filled with awe at your wonders;
where morning dawns, where evening fades, you call
forth songs of joy."

(PSALM 65:8 NIV)

When I was eight, older boys from church invited me to go hunting. With a brown paper grocery bag and a wooden stick, I'd be able to capture "snipes," small, flightless birds.

One of the boys explained that if I struck the bag and screamed, "Here snipey, snipey," the disoriented fowl would make its way into the opening.

Another instigator explained that if I wanted to apprehend this elusive bird, I'd need to go further into the forest— away from lights and people.

As I stepped deeper into the trees, the older boys said that they planned to stay behind to draw out the snipes. So I advanced into the darkness with nothing more than a grocery bag, a stick, and my naiveté.

Standing alone in the darkness, it finally struck me—the older boys were playing a trick on me. I was caught up in a foolish excursion for the entire purpose of ridicule.

All of us have been hoodwinked at one time or another. As peers spur us on, it's easy to be drawn into their games. Ridiculous claims seem more plausible when they come from our friends. We might take time to recognize the silliness of it all.

Darkness is Fading

By most measurable data, life is steadily improving around the globe. Darkness is fading, and the goodness of God's kingdom is genuinely taking root in our world.

Poverty and violence are diminishing. Evil is losing its grip on creation. The kindness of Jesus is advancing and transforming everything in its wake.

It might not seem possible, but in this era, individuals are healthier, living longer, and evading the violence of previous generations.

Across the earth, more opportunities exist than ever before. People have access to cleaner water and better food, and more equitable terms are defining relationships.

Restrictions attributed to race, gender, and social class are not as rigid as they once were. The marginalized and impoverished are finding a seat at the table. Hope is rising, and people are discovering their reason for existence. Spiritual fervor is riding high.

Summarizing his findings on global advancements, Steven Pinker recounted the following:

> The world is not falling apart. The kinds of violence to which most people are vulnerable— homicide, rape, battering, child abuse—have been in steady decline in most of the world. Autocracy is giving way to democracy. Wars between states—by far the most destructive of all conflicts—are all but obsolete.[1]

Sadly, a false sense of doom continues to grip many. It's unfortunate that multitudes gravitate toward bad news. Our hardwired pessimism and guilty self-flagellation sometimes obscure the fact that advancement is happening. Commenting on this, Matt Ridley writes,

---

[1.] Steven Pinker and Andrew Mack, "The World Is Not Falling Apart: Never Mind the Headlines. We've Never Lived in such Peaceful Times," *Slate* (December 2014).

The generation that has experienced more peace, freedom, leisure time, education, medicine, travel, movies, mobile phones and massages than any generation in history is lapping up gloom at every opportunity.[2]

Many can't get over the sense that our world is unraveling. Cynicism has colored their imagination. They cannot fathom the idea that their view of the cosmos is distorted. People love the lies that the media told them.

Contradicting our cataclysmic assumptions, beautiful changes are unfolding. God is at work, actively restoring his creation. A heavenly splendor is emanating across the horizon, renewing the fallen order.

Imagine how different it could be if people had a better grasp of what's transpiring. Perhaps someday we could let go of a pessimistic, doom-and-gloom worldview and grasp the good news of the gospel.

Embracing this enveloping hope doesn't mean a denial of problems. Goodness is advancing, but we occasionally have to wrestle with disappointment. Life is improving, but it's still not perfect. We need to even more of the goodness and grace of Jesus. We need light to shine in the midst of the darkness.

[2.] Matt Ridley, *The Rational Optimist: How Prosperity Evolves* (San Francisco: HarperCollins, 2010), 291.

Awaiting the Fullness of the Kingdom

I didn't know that this was possible, but a longtime friend warned that I was becoming too optimistic. He was convinced that my focus on the present work of Christ caused me to pay too little attention to the future.

I explained to him that while pressing into everything God is doing, I also eagerly await the ultimate culmination of his kingdom. Not all aspects of his dominion are currently manifested. The future holds a more magnificent display of glory. All of us have to navigate a realm that has been inaugurated but not consummated.

Jesus puts it like this: "The time has come at last—the kingdom of God has arrived. You must change your hearts and minds and believe the good news" (Mark 1:15 J.B. Phillips).

Even though more is on the way, that shouldn't cause us to miss what's already here. Why would anyone want to ignore what Jesus is doing in this hour? The magnificence of his awe-inspiring goodness encourages us.

Centuries ago, Jesus reassured his followers that he would sit "on his glorious throne in the renewed creation" (Matthew 19:28 ISV). He wanted them to know that the earth was being brought back into its original purposes. Old things were being renovated as he advanced in power.

The Apostle Peter uttered something similar. He noted that the ancient prophets envisioned an era of renewal. They saw a Messianic age breaking into time and history. Its disclosure would transpire after "the restoration of all things has taken place" (Acts 3:21 NLT).

In each of these accounts, it's clear that the world is racing toward something beautiful. Astounding realities are at hand. Instead of devastation, God is bringing restoration. Although we have seen many improvements, we are anticipating even more.

With Jesus's institution of the new covenant, the created order will never collapse. The world isn't getting worse. With the proliferation of mercy, the broken fragments are coming back together.

God's dominion is animating every segment of creation. Like yeast permeating a batch of dough, grace is infiltrating the economic, social, and governmental structures of our world. Societies once ravaged by darkness are regaining hope.

The earth continues to advance because the gospel is taking root in every corner of the globe. The more grace envelopes the earth, the better the world becomes. The Prophet Isaiah reminded us centuries ago,

> The government will be upon his shoulder, and his name is called Wonderful Counselor, Mighty God, Everlasting Father, and Prince of Peace. Of the increase of his government and peace, there will be no end (Isaiah 9:6b-7a ESV).

The escalation of beauty in creation will continue to grow. Men and women must put away our dreadful perspectives and embrace the wonder of a profoundly better world.

FOR FURTHER READING:

If you would like to study this topic further, works are available that examine changing world conditions and provide in-depth statistical analysis.

Improving Global Conditions

Bailey, Ronald. *The End of Doom: Environmental Renewal in the Twenty-first Century*. New York: St. Martin's Press, 2015.

Bettmann, Otto. *The Good Old Days—They Were Terrible! New York*: Random House, 1974.

Deaton, Angus. *The Great Escape: Health, Wealth, and the Origins of Inequality*. Princeton: Princeton University Press, 2013.

Easterbrook, Gregg. *It's Better Than It Looks: Reasons for Optimism in an Age of Fear*. New York: Hachette Book Group, 2018.

Easterbrook, Gregg. *The Progress Paradox: How Life Gets Better While People Feel Worse.* New York Random House, 2004.

Kenny, Charles. *Getting Better: Why Global Development Is Succeeding—And How We Can Improve the World Even More.* New York: Basic Books, 2012.

Norberg, Johan. *In Defense of Global Capitalism*, trans. Roger Tanner and Julian Sanchez. Washington, D.C.: Cato Institute, 2003.

Norberg, Johan. *Progress: Ten Reasons to Look Forward to the Future.* United Kingdom: One World Publications, 2016.

Pinker, Steven. *Enlightenment Now: The Case for Reason, Science, Humanism, and Progress*, New York: Viking, 2018.

Pinker, Steven. *The Better Angels of Our Nature: Why Violence Has Declined.* New York: Viking, 2011.

Radelet, Steven. *The Great Surge: The Ascent of the Developing World.* New York: Simon & Schuster, 2015.

Ridley, Matt, *The Rational Optimist: How Prosperity Evolves.* San Francisco: HarperCollins, 2010.

Rosling, Hans, with Ola Rosling, and Anna Rosling Rönnlund, *Factfulness: Ten Reasons We're Wrong About the World—and Why Things Are Better Than You Think.* New York, Flatiron Books, 2018.

Thomas, Chris D. *Inheritors of the Earth: How Nature Is Thriving in an Age of Extinction.* New York: Public Affairs, 2017.

The Expansion of Christianity

Balcombe, Dennis. *China's Opening Door: Incredible Stories of the Holy Spirit at Work in One of the Greatest Revivals in Christianity.* Lake Mary, Florida: Charisma House, 2014.

Doyle, Tom, with Greg Webster. *Dreams And Visions: Is Jesus Awakening The Muslim World?* Nashville: Thomas Nelson, 2012.

Garrison, David. *A Wind In The House Of Islam: How God Is Drawing Muslims Around The World To Faith In Jesus Christ.* Monument, Colorado: WIGTake Resources, 2014.

Jacob, Grace. *Dragon Ride: True Stories of Adventure, Miracles, and Evangelism from China.* Maricopa, Arizona: XP Publishing, 2017.

Jenkins, Phillip. *The New Faces of Christianity: Believing the Bible in the Global South.* New York: Oxford University Press, 2006.

Jenkins, Phillip. *The Next Christendom: The Coming of Global Christianity.* New York: Oxford University Press, 2011.

Koschorke, Klaus, Frieder Ludwig, Marian Delgado, Roland Spliesgart, and Mariano Delgado, editors. *A History of Christianity in Asia, Africa, and Latin America, 1450-1990: A Documentary Sourcebook.* Grand Rapids: Eerdmans, 2007.

Martin, David. *Tongues of Fire: The Explosion of Protestantism in Latin America.* Cambridge, Massachusetts: Blackwell, 1993.

Rosenberg, Joel C. *Inside the Revival: Good News and Changed Hearts Since 9/11*. Carol Stream, Illinois: Tyndale Publishers, 2009.

Stark, Rodney, and Xiuhua Wang. *A Star in the East: The Rise of Christianity in China*. West Conshohocken, Pennsylvania: Templeton Press, 2015.

Stark, Rodney. *Triumph Of Faith: Why The World Is More Religious Than Ever*. Wilmington: Intercollegiate Studies Institute, 2015.

Stark, Rodney. *Why God?: Explaining Religious Phenomena*. West Conshohocken, Pennsylvania: Templeton Press, 2017.

Trousdale, Jerry. *Miraculous Movements: How Hundreds of Thousands of Muslims Are Falling in Love with Jesus*. Nashville: Thomas Nelson, 2012.

QUESTIONS FOR REVIEW AND GROUP DISCUSSION

The following questions are designed to encourage review and discussion of the material in *Why You've Been Duped into Believing that the World is Getting Worse*. This section can be used for personal development or group study.

1. How does the media, government, and popular culture affect how you see the world? Why are powerful people trying to shape public opinion?

2. Does your worldview affect your identity and the way that you relate to others? If so, how?

3. Is it more advantageous to be hopeful or filled with despair? What are the practical implications of each perspective?

4. Think of some of the ways that a greater sense of hope might impact your life? Write a few of them down.

5. Describe how you will minimize negative influences? What specific actions will you take in the next thirty days?

6. If God is at work in the world, what happens? What does "good news" look like around the globe?

7. What does popular culture misunderstand about Christianity? What is the church actually up to in the world?

8. How does Christianity intersect with money, health, and family life? What are the practical implications of biblical faith?

9. Do global advancements change our outlook? Take a moment and consider what's possible?

10. If we're moving toward the renewal of creation, what should we expect to see in the future? What lies over the horizon?

11. How do you share positive developments with people who are pessimistic? How do we help people navigate the intense feelings rooted in their present worldview?

12. When we encounter short-term setbacks in our personal lives, how should we respond? What should our attitude be toward adversity?

13. Consider what's possible now—in light of the goodness and mercy of Jesus? What do you want to see happening in your day-to-day walk?

14. How will you approach the future in light of present-day advancements? What will this look like as we step into the great unknown?

About J.D. King

J.D. King was a supporting leader in the Smithton Outpouring in the late 1990s. Since then he has also served as an author, pastor, and itinerate speaker.

King spent sixteen years studying the background and theological foundations of healing. The culmination of his research is a three-volume book series called: *Regeneration: The Complete History of Healing in the Christian Church.*

In addition to writing, King guides leaders at the Revival Training Center and serves as a pastor at World Revival Church in Kansas City, Missouri.

To find out more about J.D. and how he could speak to your group, visit him online:

Email: jdking@wrckc.com
Blog: http://authorjdking.com
Bookstore: https://theresurgencestore.com
Twitter: http://twitter.com/jdkinginsights
Facebook: https://www.facebook.com/authorjdking
Newsletter: http://eepurl.com/cVCdQ5

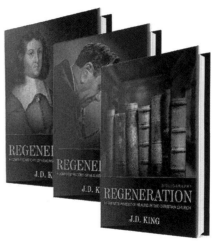

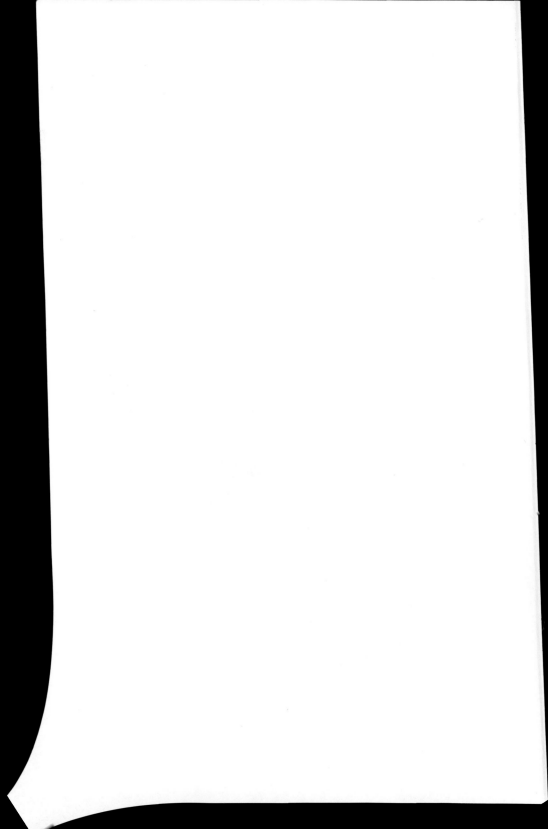

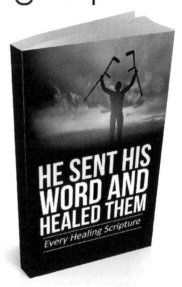

YOU CAN HELP!

Most people don't spend time reviewing items they like. They only write reviews when they are dissatisfied. What you might not know is how valuable a one-sentence review is to an author. It is like gold. If this book helped you, and I hope it has, would you please leave an honest review on *Amazon*?